wi
wl

The Recovery of Ideals

By the same author

THE RESOURCES OF RELIGION
HOLY FLAME (verse)
JOHN CALVIN: THE MAN AND HIS ETHICS
CONFLICTS IN RELIGIOUS THOUGHT

The * * * * RECOVERY OF IDEALS

By

GEORGIA HARKNESS

Professor of Philosophy in Elmira College

CHARLES SCRIBNER'S SONS · NEW YORK
CHARLES SCRIBNER'S SONS · LTD · LONDON
1937

To

three small nephews
ERNEST, CHARLES AND RALPH
harbingers of the future

PREFACE

THE purpose of this book is to suggest an empirical approach to a social philosophy and to a philosophy of religion. Its starting-point is human thinking and living as we find it in the contemporary scene. Its aim, however, is not to present one more analysis of current attitudes, of which there have been many. Its procedure rests on the conviction that in the present social outlook are imbedded permanent tendencies of human nature with which certain permanent elements of ethical and religious truth are correlative.

An empirical approach to both religion and morals seems to me to be obligatory for two reasons. The first is that neither the spiritual nor ethical idealism needed for inner stability can be imparted to others on a dogmatic basis. Thinking people in our day—particularly thinking young people—will not listen to any authoritarian "thus saith—," whether it is "thus saith the Lord," or parent, or preacher, or teacher. Without leaving our own experience behind, we must help people to discover out of their experience—unstable welter though it may be—some substantial ground on which to stand.

The second reason for an empirical approach is that if it were still possible, as in the past, to approach religion and morals from the standpoint of a completed framework of ideas, it is doubtful whether we should be justified in doing so. Both religion and morals are rooted in living, only secondarily in thought, and thought must follow the indices and pointers set up by life before it can give direction to life. This does not mean rejection of the great creedal heritage of religious thought, or the less compact but equally great inheritance of ethical speculation. Having once been confronted by these, one cannot get away from them unless he chooses to throw away his birthright. But one can avoid being controlled by them to the point of making his heritage a Procrustean bed.

The book will have much to say about ideals. This does, and does not, mean that its position is one of metaphysical idealism. As the reader will discover in Chapter XIII, my own philosophical position, though mediated to me through the idealistic heritage and retaining many of its major tenets, is probably to be classified more accurately as a form of theistic realism. I am convinced that the line of demarcation between the idealists who believe in grappling with life as it is and the realists who believe in spiritual values grows increasingly thin. My first teacher of philosophy, Professor J. E. Creighton, once published an article with the suggestive title, "Philosophy as the Art of Affixing Labels." With the fixing of labels, either to myself or others, I am very little interested. But with the discovery of true grounds on which one may believe in and live by moral and spiritual ideals I am greatly concerned. In fact, I believe it to be the major demand of the philosophic enterprise—a project so great as to make matters of diction and classification unimportant except as means to the achievement of an end.

In its general empirical underpinning, the book is concerned with the attitudes widely prevalent in "all sorts and conditions of men,"—old as well as young, illiterate and tutored. Its analysis, however, is based more specifically on an examination of the attitudes of young people. This is partly because my professional relations have thrown me most in contact with the latter group, partly because the major content of the book was originally given in lecture form before a group of adult leaders of student life and thought. However, there is justification on wider grounds for making this approach. Student thinking reflects the backgrounds of thought and attitude from which students come; student thinking will mold the thought life and attitudes of the future.

For those who like short-cuts, it may be in order to suggest that they will find a summary in the last chapter. The first half of the book is brought together at the end of Chapter VIII. The discussions of the existence and nature of God and the problem of evil are summarized at the end of the tenth and beginning of the fourteenth chapters.

To Mr. E. A. Yarrow of the Hazen Foundation I am indebted for the invitation to give a series of six addresses before the Hazen Eastern Conference in August, 1936. This brought the book into being, but since that time it has been largely rewritten and much new material added. I am grateful to Professor Edgar S. Brightman, Professor Paul Tillich, and Reverend Emmett W. Gould who have read the manuscript in full, and to a number of other friends who have given me the benefit of their disagreements on Chapter XIII. Mrs. Clifford L. Stanley has helped me with efficient secretarial assistance.

GEORGIA HARKNESS.

CONTENTS

CONTENTS

CONTENTS

The Recovery of Ideals

Chapter I

THE DISSOLUTION OF IDEALS

BACK in 1923, A. E. Wiggam wrote in *The New Decalogue of Science,* "If hope and courage go out of the lives of common men it is all up with social and political civilization."[1] These words were uttered at a time when hope and courage were on the up-tide. A great war was over, a minor business depression was safely weathered, prosperity was coming in with a full surge, and the Great God Science with its new Ten Commandments seemed about to save everybody.

The years since that time have demonstrated more graphically than any former period in history the futility of worshipping any lesser god than Jehovah. The hope and courage without which social and political civilization are doomed have been sought through artificial prosperity and artificial restoratives applied when prosperity fell ill, through technology and technocracy, through brain trusts and the schemes proposed by economic demagogues. The hope and courage of common men refuse to be denied, and in time of jeopardy any support, however fragile, is eagerly seized upon. Likewise in high places of educational eminence there is a naïve confidence that, given time enough, social studies will set the world

[1]*Op. cit.,* p. 262.

right again. Meanwhile in spite of some restoration of economic security and spread of social knowledge, the inner life of man keeps getting more insecure and not much more scientific.

I. THE LOST GENERATION

Our chief interest in this study is not with the economic order, but with the mental states of those who must live in it. What I shall say is applicable in large measure to old and young, but since these words are addressed primarily to leaders of youth I shall have in mind chiefly those persons of high school and college age, and a few years beyond, who constitute what has come to be called "the lost generation."

The unemployment picture is too familiar to require much presentation. Of those who have finished college, many with Phi Beta Kappa keys are cranking out gasoline at filling stations, while the girls they would like to marry are taking tips as hotel waitresses or working behind counters in ten-cent stores. Those whose lack of ability or good fortune denies them even this meager economic foothold live at home for the most part, often in the midst of tension because they are treated as—or at least they feel themselves to be—an economic liability to their parents. One of the most serious aspects of the problem is the thousands of youth, educated and otherwise, who are hitch-hiking or hopping freight-cars about the country as transients, being shoved along from one community to any other which will receive them.[2]

[2]Cf. Maxine Davis, *The Lost Generation,* pp. 244 ff.

In such a squirrel-cage, it is a bit farcical to talk of hope and courage. Yet we must. If these "lost" youth are to find moorings, it is as important that mental and spiritual attitudes be adapted to the strain as that economic security be established. With inner adequacy one may stand up under much economic confusion; with inner confusion no economic readjustment is adequate.

It is a truism which scarcely needs restating—yet must be constantly reiterated as a basis for procedure—that the most serious aspect of current affairs is not an economic depression but a depression in *morale*. This depression in morale has still a long way to go, I believe, before it reaches the depths at which civilization will actually collapse. Human nature has great natural resilience. But unless reconstructive forces prove adequate to checking this decline in morale the trend is bound to continue downward. It is not a thing to be charted in graphs like market reports, but it is to be discerned by plenty of empirical evidence.

Various studies have been made of the way in which our youth react to their economic plight. Maxine Davis, using the case method of talking personally to hundreds of young people in all kinds of situations, presents her findings in *The Lost Generation*. Her conclusions are summarized compactly in one of her section headings, "Mope-hope-grope." The June, 1936, issue of *Fortune* gives the results of a comprehensive study of the state of mind of youth in college, based on attitudes expressed in college papers, questionnaires and conversations with investigators. The general impression gathered from the

3

report is one of growing conservatism about challenging the social order, an increase in knowledge of social studies but not in application of them, and a general diffusion of cultural interests in which religion has a very limited place. The large-scale survey projected by the American Youth Commission when it is completed will give much more exact data than are available through either of these studies.

Until we have the results of this survey before us, the testimony of young people themselves or of those who live with them will have to be the primary source of knowledge as to what the contemporary scene is doing to their outlook on life. Even if statistical data were at hand, we should still have to exercise judgment in drawing conclusions. (Surveys are frequently most valuable in giving figures by which to prove what we know already!) Personal judgment is always in danger of falling into the fallacy of hasty generalization. However, I venture to suggest the following analysis of dominant personal attitudes, intending what is said to apply to youth in general and not exclusively to college students.

2. PREVAILING STATES OF MIND

With wide overlapping, our youth might be classified according to prevailing social and religious attitudes in five groups.

(1) First, there are the cheerful traditionalists, usually found in homes where there is still money for an occasional beef-steak, and no retrenchment on gasoline. Like their elders these think the depression can't last forever,

and things are going to be better sooner or later. As for themselves, there is not much to do now except work in an A. and P. store or drive a delivery truck, but something is bound to turn up.

They would like to get married. Some do, and take the risk of finding a way to get along, either from a job or from parents. Others defer marriage, consoling themselves, perhaps, with the thought that society is no longer mid-Victorian with regard to what happens before marriage.

To the majority of this first group, religion is practically meaningless. It has disappeared from their lives more through indifference than outright rejection. Asked their opinion, they will tell you in one form of diction or another that religion is bunk, though all right for anybody who likes that sort of thing. One evidence of this fading interest is the fact that religion no longer occupies the central place, with sex, which it once held in extracurricular "bull sessions." Some still have religious problems, but the majority seem not to think about religion enough to be troubled. To a small minority among them, religion still has personal meaning, either of the fundamentalist or liberal stamp according to their background. But in general, religion as a vital interest is defunct and the church is held either in disregard or derision. The substitute for religion is to be a good sport, take one's knocks without complaining, and wait for something to turn up.

In this group, which embraces a very large number of our youth, there is hope and courage of a sort. They are cheered by a kind of Micawber-like optimism, and this should not be discredited, for without it they would be much worse off. But in their attitudes there is not much evidence of moral or spiritual idealism. Nor is there much social realism, even after four years spent in a college where the social sciences dominate the curriculum.

(2) A second, very much smaller, group is made up of young Communists, or at least potential Communists. Not many of them understand Communism well enough, or are sufficiently committed to its ideals, to be real Communists: but they are left-wing radicals and potential revolutionists. Their number varies from nothing in the rural communities and small hinterland colleges to a large showing in New York City. Most of them would be hard to label, but they are ready to follow a leader into violent social change if the leader should emerge. This group would grow rapidly if magnetically led; for many others now in a state of complete political lethargy would be swept into revolution if they saw any prospect of success. They would be swept into Fascism as easily as into Communism, and there is much more prospect that they will be.

(3) Another small group, the social idealists, is comprised of those who see the need of non-violent social change and who have some sense of personal mission to bring it about. These, for the most part, have been indoctrinated by liberal teachers, and here and there by a socialist minister. There is often, though not always, in this group a good deal of spiritual vitality as well as social conscience, as is manifest at almost any youth conference

6

where both the personal and social aspects of religion are brought clearly into the foreground.

This third group is a small, but precious, "holy remnant." Not many such are found in colleges, and still fewer outside of college where the economic system has a better chance to get its teeth in them. The bogey spread abroad by the Hearst newspapers and other steadiers of the capitalistic ark, to the effect that colleges are hot-beds of radicalism, would be funny if it did not give rise to "gag-laws" and the economic tyranny of trustees over high-minded professors. A story which suggests how far from radicalism they are is told of a leader at a student conference who thought some economic realism ought to be introduced into an otherwise too conventional program, and who therefore broached to one of the student chairmen the idea that a place be made for a discussion of the class struggle. The reply was, "That might be a problem on some campuses, but on ours the classes get along fine!"

(4) A fourth group might be called the church loyalists, though no sharp dividing line is to be drawn between its members and those of whom I have spoken as possessing religious vitality in the first and third groups. The characteristic which distinguishes them is that they have come up through the church, still remain loyal to it, often work in it, and in general carry along the patterns of thought which their church has stood for. How effectively they do this varies greatly, with a variation depending on themselves, the church, and the community in which they live. The fact that this fourth group is of

7

considerable proportions, together with the fact that in such movements as "Christian Youth Building a New World" it tends to merge with the third, is the primary ground for hope that the church will survive. The church group is much larger outside of the colleges than within —a fact which is correlatively ominous for the future of both institutions.

(5) The preceding groups maintain hope in something —either the old order or a new one—and by such hope keep up their courage. The final group, perhaps the largest, though figures are unavailable and would be useless if we had them, are superficially cheerful but drably hopeless in the deeper areas of life. Into this group those in the others tend to pass, either by gradual stages, or by a sudden leap as some crisis shatters former moorings. These have no vocational hope, for they see nothing ahead but dead-end jobs if any; no political hope, for they are convinced that the country is run by politicians against whom the people are wholly helpless; no religious hope, for the foundations of an older faith have rotted away and fallen from under them. Their philosophy is summed up in "What's the use?" or "So then, what?", interspersed with an occasional, "Oh, yeah?"

It is of these that Miss Davis writes:[3]

They are without faith and without belief. They are skeptical of the old-fashioned religions and the rewards of the old-fashioned virtues of thrift and industry. Their lives are without spiritual meaning. Youth wants to believe. A crusader, however subversive, who reveals to

[3] *Op. cit.,* p. 369. By permission The Macmillan Co.

them a cause might find them ardent converts. . . .

This generation does not think. While the level of intelligence is high, it is atrophied with inactivity. . . . They take what they like of what they hear, and reject by instinct rather than reason. We need no clairvoyant to foretell what this tendency might mean under unscrupulous leadership.

Laying aside attempts at classification, never very successful when applied to many-sided human beings, let us see where these facts bring us. If the foregoing analysis is correct this is a not very encouraging, yet not wholly depressing, picture of the states of mind discernible in our youth. There is not much in it of the spirit of high adventure which used to make commencement orators tell them they were "the hope of the world." Some orators still tell them this, but they know it is simply part of the fol-de-rol which goes with commencement—to be packed away in moth-balls with their caps and gowns.

There is not much in it of the religious vision and devotion which made the older generation thrill to the challenge to participate in "the evangelization of the world in this generation." This was an over-optimistic challenge, but it roused many to real heights of consecrated devotion to an ideal. Among the persons who responded to it were not only those who became missionaries, but a considerably larger number who were quickened to more effective Christian service in this country. If a roster were taken of our present religious leadership of the age of forty and onward, a very large number would be found to have been formerly Student Volunteers. This specific challenge could afford to pass if another of equal effectiveness were replacing it.

It is of serious import to ask whether this is taking place. My observation leads me to answer mainly in the negative. Some of our youth, in the colleges and outside, are finding what is perhaps a correlative challenge in the enterprise of abolishing war, racial exclusiveness, or economic injustice. Idealism has not gone out; and it is to be prized as a precious possession where we find it, perhaps the more precious because of its scarcity. But no large number give evidence of being gripped by either social or religious passion.

It is not merely the absence of high response to the challenge of a cause which is alarming; even more ominous is a general undermining of a sense of responsibility. This shows itself in a fairly general expectancy that things will be *done for* a person. Deans who have to consider great numbers of applications for scholarships from persons who are indignant at the suggestion that they should render any service in return will understand what I mean. The statements of employers are, like those of all other human beings, subject to the distortion of self-interest, but there may be something in it when they testify quite generally that young people are more anxious to get positions than to perform the detailed, often monotonous and unexhilarating tasks which are involved in the execution of the duties of these positions. In short, something has happened which has greatly sapped the power of self-discipline and has put the emphasis generally on the claiming of rights rather than the acceptance of duties.

The finding of moral alibis is of course not the prerogative of any one generation. It goes back to the childhood of the race, and there is no more graphic statement of it anywhere than in the story of Adam and Eve and the serpent. But it grows increasingly common in a social order saturated with the blame-fixing habit. The depression is the cause of so many aberrations that it becomes the scape-goat for more. When a student asked me recently if I could tell her what people meant when they talked about sin and I mentioned as a rather elementary example of sin being disagreeable to one's room-mate, her reply was characteristic of a pervasive mental attitude, "Well, if we're cranky it's not our fault—it's the depression!"

The present generation of youth is neither better nor worse than any former generation, but it is more confused. It is a bewildered, shellshocked, "lost" generation, pitied and but feebly served by an almost equally bewildered and confused older generation. All want jobs, unless the natural vitality of life has seeped out of them through too much disappointment or too much charity; and they want jobs to satisfy the natural human impulse to be useful as well as to satisfy their economic needs. They want to marry and have children, and they want to see some light ahead for their children. But they see little light for themselves, either vocationally or spiritually. There is still a chance to dance, and jest, and banter each other, and what there is a chance to do, they do. This helps to keep up their courage and occupy attention so that they will not need to think too much. If they drug themselves with pleasures—movies, sex thrills, alcohol and fast motors—it is mainly because they are trying to find the "escape" of which the psychiatrists have made us conscious in recent years. Yet the effort is rather fruitless. An almost perfect symbol is the fact that they keep turning the radio dial to try to find something lively, but the atmospheric conditions are bad and the static keeps blaring in raucously through forced jokes and sentimental crooning.

What ails these youth fundamentally—and to a large degree their elders—is that they have no center of stability in their lives. The old moorings are gone and no new ones have been found. Hope and courage have not gone out of the lives of common men, but they are ebbing. When they go, the game will be up for social and political civilization. But more imminent and therefore more serious is the fact that it is *already* up for great numbers of individuals in contemporary life.

Chapter II

CAUSES AND REMEDIES

I. HOW THE DISSOLUTION CAME ABOUT

THE main purpose of this book is to suggest the outlines of a constructive philosophy of life. But before going ahead to try to discover it, we must look back to see what causes, other than the obvious one of the depression, have brought about the present situation. Some are rooted in events and conditions which cannot be changed; others, being themselves ideological, are subject to modification through other ideas. As Epictetus long ago advised,[1] we must discern clearly what is, and what is not under our control, accept the inevitable and change the alterable.

Canvassing the causes of the current depression of morals and morale, we come first upon the fact that the present generation of youth are war babies. Most of those now in college were born while the war was in progress. These and their younger brothers and sisters have all been

[1]*Encheiridion*, §1. "Make it, therefore, your study at the very outset to say to every harsh external impression, 'You are an external impression and not at all what you appear to be.' After that, examine it and test it by these rules which you have, the first and most important of which is this: Consider whether the impression has to do with the things which are under our control, or with those which are not under our control; and, if it has to do with some one of the things not under our control, have ready to hand the answer, 'It is nothing to me.' "

13

reared in an atmosphere so different from that which surrounded the childhood of their adult leaders that the person is rare who can even approximately put himself in their place to view life as they view it. They grew up in homes saturated with cynicism bred by the war, and enlivened but not elevated by the compensatory frothiness which followed. In such an environment it is not strange that their native idealism has had hard sledding.

A second factor, already implied, is that their most impressionable childhood years were those of the jazz decade. When not only big brothers and sisters but parents took to drinking and staying out nights; when a new car every year became a social necessity, and in it one could speed to a distant road-house away from social scrutiny or park unobserved by the side of a lonely highway, it is not surprising that the sins of the fathers and elder brothers were visited on the children. "True confession" magazines replaced the dime novels of an earlier day, and to "sex stuff" must be added the crime and gangsterism constantly portrayed in movies and chirruped about in radio skits. Add to these matters of personal morals the subtler influences, in home, school, screen, and printed page, of the ever-present economic scramble in a period when "Whirl was king, having driven out Zeus," and it is easy to see how the disintegration of ideals among an older generation left a baneful legacy to the one which was emerging.

Many of these youth, also, are the victims of certain types of progressive education. I use the term "victim" advisedly, with a recognition that they are also the recipients of the benefits of such education. In many respects they were better taught than were their parents, whose teachers knew less of child psychology and scientific method. But in the attempt to adapt instruction to individual interests and make the educative process pleasant, there has been much coddling. A "happy adjustment" does not always lead to disciplined living and the generation of moral responsibility. I do not mean to suggest that the hickory stick ought to return to the classroom. But I once heard an old teacher say—and I think he spoke truly—" 'There's your lessons—now git 'em' is worth more than a lot of modern pedagogy!" A sense of obligation to pursue one's task, pleasant or otherwise, has a pedagogical as well as a moral value not always found in the more enticing methods of the present and recent past.

Another contributor to the dissolution of ideals is no recent development, but its cumulative effect is more evident now than formerly. This is the banning of all religion from the schools in order that no particular religion might have a special prerogative. In a day when a considerable amount of religious instruction, and with it character training, could be expected to come from the home and church, its lack in the public school system was less serious. Now, with the disappearance of religion from many homes and the almost complete break between these homes and the church, nothing in the way of religious instruction is left for the children of these homes. The result is that they grow up young pagans.

When these children reach high school, and still more

when they reach college, there are other forces contributing to the dissolution of ideals. Perhaps the most potent is the whirl of activities, academic and social, which preempt one's life and leave no time or attention for serious thought. Sports, fraternities, and other organizations are educative factors, but educative in the direction of social conformity rather than the building of independent character.

Within the curriculum the tendency to specialization and in particular, specialization in those fields where only objective, verifiable evidence will be accepted, has had a narrowing effect on breadth of vision. By indirection, rather than by direct attack, the scientific spirit has been the foe of religion by creating the impression that there is nothing in religion worth considering. With the dissolution of religious vitality has gone the dissolution of ideals.

This is intimately related to several other factors in the method and content of the curriculum—among them the tendency to replace the liberal arts with technical and vocational training. Classical education, often stigmatized for its remoteness from life's experiences, used nevertheless to convey, along with much that was formal, much also that made for the enlargement of personal vision. It is now surrendering before the claims of a type of training which teaches people how to do things without imparting a purpose for doing them. As a result we have more technically trained people than society can possibly take care of without a social reconstruction which technology itself is unable to bring to pass.

In the liberal arts colleges, there is an overweening trust in analysis at the expense of synthesis and synopsis.[2] An evidence of this is the rather pathetic way in which scientific education, psychology, and sociology ring the ranges on "integration," doing so usually in complete disregard of life's greatest integrating force. Integration has become the shibboleth of a far from integrated educational system and an almost disintegrated society.

In higher education there is, in general, a woeful lack of correlation between instruction and life. The teacher who tries to develop in his students a realistic sense of the obligations of social living in the areas of race, war, sex, or economics is likely to be stigmatized by his colleagues as a propagandist, and by those in high places as a menace to the institution. Against such obstacles it takes courage to speak the truth as one sees it—and the moral fiber of the instructor, being thus undercut, does not impart much moral passion to the students.

Yet, somewhat paradoxically, the social sciences are among the most heavily elected courses. There are two reasons for this. One is that, left free to elect as they choose, students naturally gravitate toward what seems to them pertinent to the business of living. The other reason, probably more effective, is the fact that while vocational demand is limited everywhere else, the demand for trained social workers is increasing. The joint result is that in most colleges the departments of sociology, economics, political science, pure and applied psychology, are getting larger and larger enrollments. On the surface

[2]*Cf.* Chapter VIII for a discussion of the synoptic approach.

17

this increased interest in the social sciences augurs an increased mastery of human relations. Actually, it depends largely on the personality of the instructor and the philosophic bent of his instruction whether this study enlarges or dwarfs the social vision of the students. Where idealism is derided as lack of objectivity and sympathy is scorned as sentimentality, the result is often a shrivelling of that spiritual vitality which, left to itself, would keep fresh through nature's vivifying forces.

Again we must look backward for a reason. Philosophic materialism is not much in vogue any longer among the greater thinkers, for the implications of the new physics and the increased acceptance of emergent evolution have tipped the scales away from the mechanical, completely determined system which formerly dominated thought. But fifteen to twenty-five years ago the situation was quite different. Behaviorism was in its heyday; the rising science of sociology asserted, not as theory but as empirical fact, a deterministic psychology and relativistic ethics; criminology and psychiatry were coming into the foreground accompanied by many unsuppressed Freudian wishes. Sin and guilt got bogged, and sank out of sight in the shifting sands of "maladjustment." The comparative study of religions was demonstrating great similarities in the terrestrial history of the various faiths, and thus casting suspicions upon any celestial origin. Meanwhile the new science of the psychology of religion, not finding God among its objective phenomena, was suggesting an idea which first haunted and then captivated many minds—that God was a mere illusion—

the rainbow-hued personification of one's own fair dreams. Professor Leuba in this period was proving to us by a questionnaire that scientists no longer believed in God; Bertrand Russell in his poignantly beautiful essay, "A Free Man's Worship," was calling upon man to put away illusion and make the most of his little day in a world where relentless matter, blind to all our strivings, rolls on its relentless way.

The point of this retrospect is simply this: that it was in this naturalistic *Zeitgeist* that most of the instructors, and most of the college-trained parents, of our youth received their higher education and formulated their philosophics. As a result, it is this which they pass on, either overtly or by implication, to the new generation. Unless it is one's primary interest to follow the trends of philosophic thought—a possibility often thwarted by a very necessary absorption of attention in the more immediate demands of one's vocation—the natural tendency is to let the intellectual climate of one's life be regulated by the presuppositions of the philosophy most dominant in one's own intellectually formative years. It is natural also that this, whether true or not, should be transmitted as truth. When one eschews metaphysics, one implicitly carries over the metaphysics of one's own early training, whether of nursery or classroom. I believe this accounts, at least in part, for the fact that materialism and determinism are far more prevalent now among psychologists and sociologists than among philosophers or physicists.

The lack of religious vitality—or even religious interest —in college faculties is notable, and gives students one of their chief alibis for passing religion by with sophisticated indifference. While religion and the church are not to be equated they are at least connected, and the fact that comparatively few of the faculty in most colleges attend church with any frequency—usually only on ceremonial occasions—has a direct effect upon the students' assumption that it is not worth while to go to church. It is not a very long step from this to the assumption that there is not very much in religion anyway; and when this is carried on to the assumption that religious sources of stability are mere "escapes," the triumph of secularism is complete.

As for the parents of the present generation, many have completely given up the search for religious moorings. Disillusion with traditional ideas has in many cases become the dissolution of religion. They feel with a vague sense of disturbance that *their* parents, out of their religion, passed on to them something they would like to transmit to their children, but they see no way to do it honestly. They send the children to Sunday school with a dull hope they may get something there, or they keep them at home to prevent their being indoctrinated with falsehood—as the case may be—and all the while present to the children the influences of a decent and cultured but thoroughly irreligious home. This is not an atmosphere in which idealism can thrive at its best.

Such a home as I have just described has usually in it still the roots of domestic stability from which emerges a more or less satisfactory type of character training. But the "broken home," broken in unity of spirit if not in outward form, presents a problem not only to the psychologist and sociologist but to the ethical idealist as well. Figures can be cited to prove the alarming degree of correlation between juvenile delinquency and broken homes. While no figures are available to prove what the disintegration of the home has done to the subtler aspects of human personality, the evidences lie around us on every side.

In canvassing the causes of the dissolution of ideals, I shall not stop long to cast aspersions upon the church.[3] It is weakened by archaic theology, authoritarian method, spiritual inertia, poor Sunday school instruction, indifference to social issues, denominational division and preoccupation with its own machinery. Students are generally avid to declare that they never learned anything in Sunday school or got any good from going to church. Yet the church is still the chief agency for the steady, week-by-week cultivation of ideals of moral living and spiritual power. With greater light and courage in its leadership, it might have done more. But God and it are to be thanked that it has not done less.

It is tragic, both for churches and colleges, that there is not more of an *entente cordiale* between these two institutions. Those in churches who charge that colleges are faith-wreckers need to be reminded that most students do not come to college with any great amount of faith to be wrecked. On the other hand, we in the colleges need to open our eyes, with candor and repentance, to the fact

[3]In *The Resources of Religion,* Chap. IV, I have discussed its elements of impotence and power.

that students who come to college with some measure of religious vitality are apt to leave with less, and with scorn of the churches in which they were nourished. There is a vicious circle, of baneful consequences, in the fact that one of the chief sources of ineptitude in the church is its desertion by the intelligentsia on the ground that it is inept. When it has failed to cultivate personal or social idealism in an effective way, one of the reasons is the fact that the college-trained have largely passed it by on the other side and then have complained of its lack of health.

War cynicism, jazz mania, an educational system in which self-discipline is minimized, a whirl of competing interests and activities, an over-specialized, over-technical, unintegrated and abstract type of higher education, the cumulative influences of theoretical materialism, declining interest in religion and the church among teachers and parents, the disintegration of the home, the inability of the church to cope with the mounting secularism of society—all these, *not singly but together,* have converged upon our youth in a day when unemployment alone would have been enough to wreck them. What is to be wondered at is not that they are baffled and confused, but that they have any foundations at all on which to stand.

2. WAYS OUT

What is to be done about it? There are several courses which may be followed, with varying possibilities of success.

The first is to keep going as we are, as well as we can,

22

and "let nature take its course." This means, in part, letting a natural human resilience inject such hope and courage as it can. But it means, in effect, maintaining the *status quo*—an economic society so full of impediments to this natural human resilience that it cannot operate very effectively except among the more privileged members. Our human nature does not like to be jogged out of its incrusted prejudices and traditionalism, it does not want the profit motive to be disturbed: but until both traditionalism and acquisitiveness are radically challenged the remedial forces in human nature are largely blocked.

Nature, left to itself, defeats nature. This means that sin is so permeating a fact of human life that we can have no blithe optimism about its being eradicated simply by giving the curative processes of nature more time to work. If there is one truth which is being driven home with insistent vigor in current theology, it is that the evolutionary optimism of the nineteenth century is disproved both by empirical fact and the insights of the Christian Gospel. "The evil which I would not, that I do," and whether it is expressed in acquisitiveness, pugnacity, the will to power, or its myriad other forms, letting nature take its course will not get us out of it.

The second way out is that of a modified environment. This may mean a large-scale reconstruction of the economic foundations of life, such as is proposed by the Marxian ideal of a classless society. Or it may mean the piece-meal but persistent reconstruction going on constantly through reform legislation, municipal projects, clinics of one sort and another, and various kinds of social work. To provide at public expense facilities for both work and play means, or at least should mean, concern for mental and physical health as well as for economic need. Whether the way of modified environment takes the form of WPA jobs, a municipal bathing beach, a tuberculosis clinic, or a shift in room-mates, the assumption is implied that if we change the outer conditions of life a corresponding change of inner outlook will take place.

Because this is a truth so self-evident, the fact that it is only a half-truth is easily obscured. Where some objective cause for an inner disturbance of personality is discovered, the obviously sensible thing is to alter the situation which has caused it. There is no need to dispute the importance of adjustment of environment to individual need. But when this way is followed to the exclusion of others, it is ineffective for three reasons.

In the first place, the environment at the crucial point of trouble is often unchangeable. Death, for example, is a fact to be accepted, and when the death of a loved person occurs no amount of changed environment will take the place of recognition of the necessity of inner readjustment to unchangeable, objective fact. Some of life's most tragic maladjustments come from refusal to face the fact that a severed limb will not grow again, that spent years will not return, that money once freely enjoyed is gone. There may be, and must be, unpleasantness in facing these facts, but there is also a vivifying challenge in the awareness that no situation, however unalterable, need inevitably daunt the human spirit.

A second reason for refusing to trust too implicitly the way of changed environment is the fact that in many situations the change, though desirable and in the long run perhaps possible, is not to be had *now* when we most need it. A philosophy of "the inevitability of gradualness," if not tied up to a theory of automatic progress, is sound. Marxian utopianism, if not trusted too naïvely or rejected too hastily, will beckon man along towards the achievement of a more equalitarian and just society. But in the present it will not help us greatly to believe that in the distant future, things will be better. Such confidence is not fruitless, for it motivates effort towards progress; but it is no substitute for present mastery of a situation.

A final reason for distrust of environmental change as fully effective to the stabilization of the inner life is the plain fact that no amount of alteration of environment will do anything for the person who lacks the inner resources to utilize the change. Whether he refuses through ignorance or obstinacy to put himself into it, or being in it refuses to let it do anything to him, the result is the same. One may write a cipher. This could be illustrated from the experience of the slum-dwellers or the *bourgeoisie,* the illiterate or the most highly educated.

A third way out of turmoil is the attempt to correct the limitations of the preceding by building up inner supports through education. Since education is a very general term which may include whatever does anything to the ideas, feelings or behavior patterns of an individual, I should probably explain that I am now speaking chiefly of the imparting of knowledge, the development of technical skills, and the widening of intellectual interests. I mean what Socrates is generally supposed to have meant when he said, "Virtue is knowledge." It is this confidence in the power of knowledge which has underlain the enormous expansion in facilities for secondary and college education in the past twenty-five years. It is this which has underlain the philosopher's and the scientist's confidence in reason for the past twenty-five centuries. It is integrated with the optimistic hope of both secular and religious liberalism that if only people knew enough, they would act rightly.

Both the pressure of events and the current theological emphasis on human sin and divine grace have been driving home to us the fallacy of this confidence in the power of knowledge. Education is indispensable: yet ideas when ungalvanized by emotion are ineffective, and ideas when made dynamic by the wrong emotions are dangerous.

For two reasons education, even when vivified by such emotions as can be imparted under the caption of "teaching appreciation," is inadequate to stabilize personal living. The first of these is that we all know what to do better than we do it. Shakespeare was right when he said, "If to do were as easy as to know what were good to do, chapels had been churches, and poor men's cottages princes' palaces." The second is that any education yet devised is unable to reach the whole personality, and the more it puts its trust in standardized tests, charts, graphs and questionnaires, the more it seems to lose the living whole. Goethe's words, though spoken in another connection, are here relevant:

> To understand the living whole
> They start by driving out the soul;
> They count the parts, and when all's done,
> Alas! the spirit-bond is gone.[4]

The fourth way out attempts to correct the third by emphasis on personal religious experience. It is not a new way, as, indeed, none of these is. However, it had fallen into decline in recent years through the competing vogue of environmental adjustment and the imparting of ideas. It is coming back, with its most forthright exponents to be found among the Oxford Groups, the Anglo-Catholics, the Friends, and the fundamentalists. These groups, widely different though they are in religious ideology and expression, have a common characteristic in making much of prayer and worship, and as a result they have in them more of religious vitality than is found elsewhere in Protestantism today.

Personal religious experience is of great worth in stabilizing life. Much of what follows in this volume will attempt to elaborate this fact. Yet it also carries with it great possibilities of harm. Three dangers, in particular, so beset the religious outlook that one must ever say, "Soul, be on thy guard."

Perhaps the most besetting is the danger of spiritual pride and pretension. Even the most religious person

---

[4]*Faust,* Part I, Act I, in *Werke,* Stuttgart, 1851, vol. XI, p. 70.

rationalizes his selfishness to the point of claiming special privilege and his egotism to the point of thinking of himself more highly than he ought to think. One's religion may have a purging effect in the direction of true humility; it may also be a subtle medium for self-glorification if one allows himself to think that he, better than another, is glorifying and serving God.

Another danger is the familiar charge of the irreligious that religion is an escape from reality. It need not be, but it often is. It is important to have individual lives changed to more God-centered channels, to be vivified by worship, to feel the presence of God. But when this way of release is taken as a substitute for social action or an intelligent grasp of the causes of things, it becomes pernicious.

The third danger which impregnates personal religion is that it may not be personal enough. Along with a vivifying emotional experience one may accept from the environment a false set of ideas, and identifying the two may lack a basis on which personally to challenge the latter and purge it of elements of untruth. This happens wherever traditionalism is held to with a rigor that defies examination. It happens also, though with less emotional warmth, in a dogmatic humanism.

The presence of these dangers does not eliminate the possibility of using religion as a ground of security. But religion, like time and nature, a changed environment or education, falls short of doing all that must be done.

The four ways out which I have indicated all have in them sources of power and elements of limitation. The

28

fifth way is the way of creative idealism. Its outlines are simple, its achievement difficult. It is the way which combines the constructive elements of all the others, avoiding the pitfalls of a too limited emphasis on one to the exclusion of the rest.

The way of creative idealism is a multiple approach— an approach which organizes in a unified, dynamic vision all that is useful and valid in other channels. It involves recognition of the genuinely curative forces of human nature, but is not blind to the power of traditionalism and sin. It uses all that psychology, sociology, economics, or technology can put forth for the removal of obstacles to nature's curative powers, but is not led into the illusion that putting poultices on the outside of sick lives will necessarily cure festering sores within. It works for an enrichment of personality through an enlargement of the range of interests and ideas, but is not guileless enough to suppose that reason or knowledge alone will lead either an individual or society into the kingdom of God. It recognizes the power of personal religion as a dynamic to triumphant living, but is equally conscious of the pitfalls which line the path of him who would follow the religious way. Doing all these things, it asserts that man cannot live with hope and courage unless he has worthy ideals by which to regulate his life with an inner authority.

3. WHY CREATIVE IDEALISM IS NECESSARY

From the standpoint of strategy, a multiple approach is necessary because no other will work. At least, no other has—and the inherent limitations of each way other than this one make it improbable that they will be much more successful in the future than hitherto. Some gaining of ground along all fronts we may expect, but unless we advance unitedly the advance in one place may mean retrogression elsewhere. There are clear evidences of the pass to which we have come because we have tried education without religion, or religion without intelligence, or social tinkering without much of either.

It may legitimately be asked whether a multiple approach with creative idealism as its key-note will work any better. There is affirmative empirical evidence. One has only to scan the record of "saints, apostles, prophets, martyrs" in history, or of those who live courageously and triumphantly in the present, to discover that an idealism grounded in a clear vision of realities does something in human living. What it does in the lives of individuals is its surest guarantee of social effectiveness, provided it unites responsibility with understanding and does not try to over-simplify the task of social reconstruction.

But the pragmatic argument is not the only reason for defending a multiple approach. It is rooted by nature in both religion and philosophy. Religion means fundamentally faith in a meaningful existence—a faith which, far more than the dicta of the creeds, has been shattered in our day. The way to recover this faith is to recognize that a meaningful existence implies *wholeness*—the integration of life about a center with radii extending in proper balance to every aspect of life. Philosophy means the attempt to think consistently about the meaning of life as a whole. The only way to do this, and not be led off into the by-ways of logic-chopping, is to recognize that life is an enterprise having many aspects which must be brought into unity by a multiple approach.

There are many centers about which one may organize his life and find some meaning in it. One may organize it about economic values, find some satisfactions, exclude what is richest, and learn the truth of the words, "What is a man profited if he shall gain the whole world and lose his own soul?" He may organize it about power and prestige, lord it over others, and lose command of himself. He may organize it about knowledge, gaining many facts, and run the risk of losing wisdom to become an emotionally sterile pedant. He may organize it about art, grasping and mediating beauty, and perhaps make beauty a substitute for both righteousness and holiness. He may organize it about human love, gaining and giving enlargement of life, but always he faces conflicts among his objects of devotion and is in peril of letting his love become calculating and prudential. Only life which has a religious center is organized about an unconditioned and ultimate meaning, and only in religion which is purged of distorted vision do we have genuine integration of spirit.

No human life is thus completely organized and purged. But to the degree that we approximate it, we live the life of creative idealism. With such a vista, life gets a sense of direction and the ability to steer by it towards a goal.

Chapter III

THE PLACE OF IDEALS IN HUMAN NATURE

IN THE preceding chapter we examined some of the processes which have contributed to the shattering of ideals in our time. We shall now look at some of the deeper and more permanent elements in the situation, and shall hope thus to find clues pointing toward a way of reconstruction.

We shall begin by examining the nature of man. This procedure is based on the simple pedagogical principle of going from the known to the unknown. Man's existence is indubitable; about his nature we do not know everything, but we know by experience a great deal. If we say we have certainty of God or of the cosmic status of ideals we speak with insufficient caution, and whatever degree of certainty we do possess comes through our knowledge of man, the workings of the human spirit, and our convictions as to man's place in the cosmos.[1]

The most dominant characteristic of man is that he is a citizen of two worlds. Original sin and original goodness contend within him; so likewise do finitude and infinity.

[1] I do not deny revelation. But revelation is meaningless apart from a knowledge of man's capacity to receive it.

I. ORIGINAL SIN AND ORIGINAL GOODNESS

By original sin I do not mean just what St. Augustine and the orthodox Christian tradition have meant by it. The Babylonian epic of the fall of man, adopted by Semitic tradition and narrated with moral beauty in the third chapter of Genesis, mixed by Augustine with the Platonic myth of man's pre-existence in a supramundane world of perfect archetypes, and transmitted into the tradition of the church to be literalized into plain, prose doctrine—this myth has been the source of much bad psychology and bad theology. But there is both psychological and theological truth in it which we ought not lightly to disregard.

Psychological study gives plenty of evidence of man's inherent tendency to sin, if we are not afraid to let a much shunned word into our terminology. Any realistic view of childhood will see there traces of "original sin" in the ever-present tendency of the child to *demand, demand,* then *demand more* of a sick, tired mother, or of any one who is accessible for the satisfaction of desires. Children by nature are egocentric little animals, with a dominant concern to obtain for themselves a maximum of satisfaction. A child does not need to be taught to grab another child's toys, or to defend his own from aggression. One does not have to be around a three-year-old long to discover that "That's mine" and "I want that" are two of the commonest expressions in his vocabulary.

Social conditioning and the emergence of altruistic tendencies tone down somewhat this fundamental selfishness. But what adult can say with honesty that he is free from it? Its roots run through the entire emotional life, mixing with pride, anger, envy, and the rest of the seven deadly sins, and many more, to corrupt our natures and distort our living. Probably its most insidious form is that tendency to rationalize the will to power which cloaks even our higher moral impulses in self-righteousness to the point of making us oblivious of its existence.

Egocentricity pursues us where we least suspect its presence, easily substantiating the belief in a personal devil. I do not, on metaphysical grounds, accept belief in such a devil, but there is everything in our psychological natures to make us feel as if we were in the grip of a power not ourselves which makes for evil. This inherent tendency to selfishness, projected from the individual into a social order made up of selfish individuals, is the root of exploitation, war, and chaos.

Selfishness is not merely self-reference. There is a good deal of popular and academic cynicism which claims that even our noblest acts of service are subtly motivated by a desire to please ourselves, and therefore reduce to selfishness. This is a half-truth which as usually stated becomes an untruth. It is true that all motivation has self-reference in it. What a motive is, is simply an urge toward the satisfaction of a desire sufficiently compelling to induce one to act. Whenever I act voluntarily, I act because I want to satisfy something in me; and I can no more be satisfied by another person's urge to the fulfilment of desire than my body can be nourished by the food another person eats. This holds of the most altruistic as well as the most selfish acts. Kagawa, like Mussolini, is driven by an urge toward the satisfaction of an impulse within his nature. But this self-reference, native to us all and inevitable, is not what I meant by sin.

Sin enters at the point where this urge toward the satisfaction of desire becomes a *narrow* and *exclusive* interest.[2] Exclusiveness, whether an exclusion of values essential to the wholeness of our own personalities or an exclusion of other persons from the range of interest, is the basic form of sin. When I will to be less of a person than I might be, I sin. When I will to secure values for myself which I am not willing to help others to secure for themselves, I sin. When I will to secure values for myself which I am not willing as far as circumstances permit to share with others, I sin. The phrase "as far as circumstances permit" is both a necessary safeguard against fanaticism and an easy door through which to escape responsibility. Presumably it is not my duty literally to sell all my goods and give the proceeds to the poor; yet I am selfish and therefore sinful when, recognizing this fact, I make it an excuse for living in comfortable indifference to the fact that thousands of human beings die annually of under-nourishment because of an unjust social order.

To illustrate again, it is not sinful to seek knowledge in order that one may be a wiser person and therefore have more to share. But to seek knowledge to the exclusion from life of health, friendship, beauty, or holiness

---

[2]Both motive and consequences need to be taken into account in judging any such interest. The subjective and objective factors in a moral decision are not identical, but an artificial separation is dangerous.

is sinful; to seek it for private gain is to make it the tool of a subtle will to power which corrupts personalities and undermines societies.

Sin enters most often in connection with economic goods because these are by nature exclusive values while wisdom, worship, friendship, and beauty are more readily shareable. But "love of money" is not "the root of *all* evil." The most insidious forms of evil are those wherein a value which by its nature is meant to be shared is hugged as a private possession. Snobbishness, whether intellectual, ecclesiastical or social, is not simply one of the most unlovely of human attitudes; it is one of the most demonic.

This tendency to the exclusive enjoyment of our own ego and its appurtenances is the permanent meaning of "original sin."[3] There is a perpetual "fall" when man, seeing the good, narrows the range of his self-satisfactions to do evil. Such a stranglehold does it have upon us all that it is not surprising that Christian theology has held redemption to be possible through divine grace alone.[4]

With the marks of original sin, we bear in us also traces of original goodness. This does not mean, as Rousseau held, that human nature left to itself will turn out all right. Romanticism like the doctrine of human depravity is a half-truth which is also at least half error.

[3]This recognition of the permeating character of our moral egotism is most incisive in the prophetic element of Hebrew-Christian faith. But even in so aristocratic a mental climate as that reflected by Plato, there is an implicit recognition of it. The Socratic-Platonic doctrine that virtue is knowledge roots in the fact that nobody will admit having willfully and maliciously done evil. *Cf.* F. J. E. Woodbridge, *The Son of Apollo*, pp. 134 f.

[4]Sin and salvation in their deeper religious significance will be discussed in Chapter XIV.

Yet the shrewdest judge of human nature who ever lived would not have set a child in the midst and said, "Of such is the kingdom of heaven," unless he had seen there elements of an inborn divinity—or, since we are not yet ready to talk about God, elements of a native moral perfection.

Wordsworth probably went beyond the bounds of psychological realism in his famous ode:

> Heaven lies about us in our infancy!
> Shades of the prison-house begin to close
>   Upon the growing Boy,
> But he beholds the light, and whence it flows,
>   He sees it in his joy;
> The Youth, who daily farther from the East
>   Must travel, still is Nature's Priest,
>   And by the vision splendid
>   Is on his way attended;
> At length the Man perceives it die away,
> And fade into the light of common day.

Taking this for what it is meant to be, not a psychologist's analysis of statistical data but an artist's vision, there is the sound of truth in these words. One must be quite lacking in discernment who does not find in the same three-year-old referred to above not only egocentricity, but intimations of a realm of spiritual reality beyond the crude attainment of either child or adult life. Children are neither little devils nor little angels, but there is in child nature something both demonic and divine.

So much of our goodness has to be "coaxed along" as

we grow to maturity that it is less easy on empirical grounds to make out a case for original goodness than for original sin. Yet none of us could achieve goodness at all, either through divine or human effort, unless goodness were in some sense native to us.

As the roots of sin are in selfishness and exclusiveness, so goodness roots in a common human tendency to project interest outward toward other human beings. It appears in the child's capacity to love and attempt to please, first those on whom he is dependent, and then a wider circle. Such other-regarding interest is less spontaneous than our egocentricity and requires much fostering: but there is in all normal human nature the capacity to be motivated by concern for the well-being of others. The degree to which it manifests itself, as well as the form of action it takes and the persons upon whom it is directed, is determined in large part by the social inheritance and in particular by early training. But the significant fact is that neither the social inheritance as a whole nor any training in particular could make us act altruistically, in opposition to powerful egoistic impulses, unless the capacity for altruism were an original endowment of human nature.

Man, whether in the relatively unmodified state of childhood, or in maturity after society and some measure of self-direction have done their work, is a mixture of original sin and original goodness. There is in him no such clearly drawn warfare between flesh and spirit as Paul and Augustine envisaged. But rooted in both flesh and spirit and manifest in both flesh and spirit, an eternal conflict between good and evil is being waged. Evil is mixed with good, and good with evil, and this very fact of mixture serves to complicate and accentuate the fact that the personality is being pulled by opposing impulses. It is a conflict so disrupting to man's nature that he must somehow find a way out of it. And because he is a human being and not simply a biological organism, he does find a way which frees him—never wholly, but in part—from the clashing currents in his members.

2. HUMAN AND ANIMAL NATURE

In this conflict between evil and good impulses, the personality has both assaults and reinforcements from without. But the issue is primarily settled by impulsions and inhibitions *from within*. As the growing personality achieves maturity and force of character, there is less and less dependence on external coercions. The fully mature person does not have to be kept in check by physical or legal sanctions, or even by public opinion, for he has learned to regulate his life from within with relative indifference to outer enticement or assault; and in acts of heroic fidelity to his own ideals he defies society to the point of accepting ostracism or death rather than compromise. That there are few such "fully mature persons" —probably no living person is completely so—does not nullify the fact that the more ethically mature a person is, the more he relies on inner rather than outer restraints.

This capacity to live by an *inner non-coercive authority* to which one yields his life is man's most distinctive trait. It is here that man differs most from the sub-human animals, whose behavior may be either attractive or perverse according to human standards, but is neither good nor evil in a moral sense. An animal reacts to a stimulus; a man responds to a situation. Such response is complex, and conscience is obviously not the only element in it. Yet it is of supreme importance that man is motivated, at least in his most *human* acts, by an inner authority which acts upon him with the power of an objective force. Though we ordinarily call it conscience, or a sense of moral obligation, it could equally well be termed the power to live by ideals.

The fundamental distinction between human and animal intelligence is often stated in terms of reason and imagination. I do not wish to deny the importance of either. Both enter into this ideal-forming, self-directive capacity. Yet it is not identical with either, for one may reason or project goals in imagination without acting. John Macmurray in his *Creative Society*[5] links the fear of death with reason as the primary human capacity unpossessed by animals, and makes this the root of religion. I believe this distinction to be overdrawn, and in any case, subordinate to the more fundamental difference that a man can definitely envisage *what he ought to do* and set himself, against the weight of conflicting impulse, *to the doing of it.* It is intimately related to reason, for it involves the human capacity to bring together past, present and future in an act of conscious thought. But it is more than a cognitive matter. It roots in a fundamental difference in the emotional life whereby human emotions

[5] *Op. cit.,* Chap. III.

take on moral significance and impel the individual to self-directed action; while animal emotion is the bare, uncontaminated and unglorified, outcropping of instinctive impulse. To be ruled by emotion in the same "un-self-directed" way the animal is, is to throw away one's human birthright and sink toward the level of the beast.

3. FINITENESS AND INFINITY

Man, then, is a mixture of good and evil, a natural endowment which is his to build upon or be crushed beneath. But we said also at the beginning of the chapter that man is a mixture of finiteness and infinity. This requires further examination.

Man in his inner life is fundamentally fearful, lonely and bewildered—a state of affairs accentuated by recent social phenomena but basically characteristic of human nature. His most fundamental impulses are sex, acquisitiveness, and the will to power.[6] With each of these impulses are mingled deep-seated, profoundly disturbing emotions.

Fear stalks its way through life introducing ghoulish specters into what might otherwise be joyous experiences. The lover fears that he—or she—may not win the object of devotion, and when the family is established fears still that loyalty may slip away. Fear besets sexual satisfaction. It engenders terror, even in a personally courageous man, at the thought of injury which may befall his family.

[6]There are, of course, many other impulses characteristic of human nature. Pugnacity may belong here as much as the three explicitly mentioned. However, these are the most elemental. Pugnacity and jealousy often appear when one of these is thwarted.

Almost everybody, whether with family responsibilities or not, fears that he may not possess enough to make his economic status certain, and having won possessions, fears that he may lose them. With economic stability relatively assured, fear of losing caste or prestige is still a haunting terror, making one feel driven by the pressure of his group, however circumscribed, to conform to its demands.

Human fear is more intense and devastating than any animal fear could be, for the reason that to biological fear is added that which comes with the enlargement of outlook and the awareness of all that is at stake. For the same reason, there is probably more fear in an advanced than in a primitive society, where in spite of many superstitious terrors now banished it was true that "ignorance is bliss." A homely example of this is the fear of germs, amounting in some almost to a mania, which possesses us today in contrast with the blithe assurance of our forefathers.[7]

Loneliness, like fear, besets man's life. The home is intended by nature to give intimate companionship, but if one may trust the testimony of many in family relations which seem on the outside to be satisfactory, it gives conjunction of clashing temperaments more often than genuine unity of spirit. Economic activities in all but the rarest of instances are divisive rather than soul-uniting agencies. The quest for power and prestige elicits social recognition but not true understanding.

Isolation, like fear, grows more devastating as man ad-

[7] A hearty old man, being asked to what he attributed his excellent health, replied that he was born before germs were discovered and therefore had had less than others to worry about.

vances. It is doubtful whether animal loneliness can compare in intensity with the human awareness of lack of inner comradeship; and the more complex society becomes, the more the individual feels himself lost in the great shuffle. The child lost in a swirling crowd of unfamiliar faces and crying for those he loves is symbolic of the experience of many adults who feel an overwhelming sense of loneliness in the presence of human indifference and nature's "great unknowns."

To fear and loneliness are linked confusion of soul. To live is to face a future of which the platitudinous "You never can tell what's going to happen next" is an apt description; while to die, for those not rooted in religious faith, is a leap in the dark which a natural biological impulse to self-preservation invests with terror.

I have referred to the importance Macmurray attaches to the fear of death, making it the basic symbol of human fear. There is no reason to deny the place which death and its correlative, the hope of immortality, have occupied in all human experience. Religion might have existed without it, but would have taken quite a different trend. Yet I doubt whether, except in the presence of imminent danger, death is dreaded by most people as much as life. Death is dreaded when one thinks about it; life has to be thought about—that is, faced and somehow grappled with—all the time. Life is feared not only because it is dangerous, but more because it is chaotic, turbulent, beset with uncertainties which may turn out to be nothing but in anticipation loom large with awful possibilities. Confronted with them, it is easy to say to another a cheerful

"Don't worry. Things will come out all right." But not many who give this advice blithely can follow it themselves.

So this is the state in which we live. A war or an economic crisis, a sudden and irreparable physical injury or a blasting of hopes may bring these turbulent emotions vividly into the foreground. But they are always in the background, lurking like the legendary three-headed Cerberus to leap upon the wayfarer. It is to these forces that even with the best of inner buttressing, we are largely subject.

I do not wish to paint an over-gloomy picture from which pleasurable satisfactions are omitted. There is plenty of joy in life: friendship, family, love, laughter, and sunsets have their place and only the dullard or misanthrope fails to find enjoyment in them. But yet however much we may desire to—and have a right to—look on the brighter side of things, it is to drug oneself with optimism if one fails to see that there is an element of original unhappiness and chaos in us all which relatively few people successfully surmount. This is the deep-lying truth in the commonplace, bitter ejaculation, "Life is hell!"

In so far as we surmount this condition, it is through ideals. This does not necessarily mean religious ideals, though it is through religious ideals that the most effective conquest comes. In so far as our idealism is thin, we are a prey to impulse and circumstance, living conventionally acceptable or socially stigmatized lives, as the accident of environment may dictate, but never living with true self-mastery. Such an existence may be a negatively tranquil but is never a genuinely happy life; it is the victim of too many evil forces pressing from within and without. Of such are the peevish, the complaining, and the bored.

It is through ideals that the element of infinity becomes operative in us, redeeming in a measure the finitude which otherwise possesses us. By infinity I do not mean any mysterious supernatural power. That there may be something of mystery in it and something above the natural I do not deny, nor is it necessary at this point to affirm it. What I mean is simply the empirical fact that human nature is so constituted that it can rise above the forces which would otherwise condemn us to live in darkness and dread—the victims of confusion and chaos. I call this capacity to surmount limitation *infinity* because, just as fear, loneliness, and bewilderment hedge us in and set barriers to our living, this capacity releases us to live victoriously in a manner to which there is no setting of upper limits.

4. THE FUNCTION OF IDEALS

Ideals, though acquired, are our natural birthright by virtue of our human heritage. Apparently no animal possesses them, and no normal human being is wholly without them. They vary both in quality and force, and in the degree to which they are higher or lower, more or less regulative, lies our escape from "hell."

There is an important difference, and at the same time no clear line of demarcation, between our escape from sin and our release from limitation. Between a bad will and a weak will—an evil deed and a foolish one—there is a real difference which needs to be preserved lest moral responsibility be lost. A person *sins* when he might do better and "misses the mark"; a person *fails* when nature or society has laid upon him burdens too grievous to be borne and he sinks beneath them.[8] Yet though it is imperative to preserve this distinction, it is equally essential to avoid any pharisaic drawing of rigid lines between the sin and the weakness of other men.

Some sin, some limitation we all must have as long as we remain human. But there is vastly more of both than is necessary. To say of any evil or weakness, "That's only human nature," is to miss the greater fact that there lies within human nature a channel of release.

It is through ideals that we discover direction and power both to resist temptation and to overcome limitation. If our ideals are as inclusive as they ought to be, we find through them not only personal mastery but the impetus toward the creation of a society where none need be inhibited by artificial barriers from living at his best. The function of ideals is both individual and social. In the power to live by ideals, whether directed against sin or chaos, lies salvation.

We are not ready yet to say whether this power is of God. It may be, yet some of the channels it takes—as we shall see presently—are quite ungodlike. The prior fact is that *ideals are*. Because they are, men live differently.

[8]Some of these limitations will be discussed in Chapter XV.

Because some ideals are both pure and potent, some men find salvation from inner catastrophe. There is no man living who can say without self-deception that his escape is absolute. Yet a road which leads even to partial salvation is of supreme worth, so long as it leads forward.

Chapter IV

THE REALITY OF THE IDEAL

IN THE preceding chapter some things were said about both the meaning and the potency of ideals. It is necessary now to examine the term more closely. It has been cast into disfavor by a common assumption that an ideal is a vague and illusory nothing-in-particular, a sort of pretty will-o'-the-wisp to lead spiritually-minded but soft-hearted and empty-headed people away from the paths of dependable realism. The most essential thing to say about the meaning of ideals is that they are among life's most dependable realities. The major proof of this is that when one acts by them, all of life is different.

1. IDEALS AND PRINCIPLES

An ideal is a certain type of principle. It is a principle accepted as a basis for future action because it has an emotional as well as a cognitive appeal. In short, an ideal is an idea made dynamic through feeling. It is a regulative value-judgment.

In every ideal there is an element of reason, memory, and imagination. These converge in the capacity which human beings have (and sub-human animals lack) to regulate action in the present by a rational synthesis of principles common to past experiences and by an imaginative projection of goals into the future. By such rational synthesis and imaginative projection a person discovers what he *can* do and *might* do. But not until he feels that he *ought* to do it, does his idea become an ideal.

An ideal is a conviction that something ought to be, held before the mind with sufficient power to motivate effort to bring it to pass. Thus we have ideals of order and harmony, of beauty, of friendship and good will, of a world without war when the lion shall lie down with the lamb and men shall beat their swords into ploughshares and their spears into pruning-hooks. These are ideals *for us* only as we think them worth putting forth effort to attain. The person who would like to see the world rid of war but whose effort does not go beyond the wishing stage does not have an ideal of world peace. Thus, there is in every ideal a volitional, as well as a cognitive and emotional, element.

2. THE ATTAINABILITY OF IDEALS

Ordinarily, in contrasting the ideal with the real, the ideal is thought of as the not-yet-attained. This element of future temporality is, so far as I can see, not an indispensable attribute. Some ideals are and some are not attained; some are and some are not attainable. The carpenter's ideal of precise craftsmanship that makes him want to set his timbers exactly straight instead of haphazardly tilted is attainable, and by the aid of a square, a spirit level, or a plumb line reality and ideality are brought into conformity. This does not mean that the ideal has vanished when attained: rather, that a regulative idea accepted as mandatory upon action has brought to pass an act, and with it an effect, which would otherwise have been different.

The case is far less simple in the field of morals, where we have no such objective measure of attainment and there are subtler forces than those of gravity with which to contend. But there is a basic similarity not to be overlooked in the recognition of differences. When one adopts an ideal—let us say, of keeping one's temper in check under irritation—he adopts a principle which he thinks ought to hold under adversity or annoyance: he believes it to be an attainment worth working for at the cost of inhibition of impulse, and with varying success he attains it. The fact that probably no human being lives who is good-tempered all the time is no more an evidence of lack of attainment than is the fact that the best-built structure in the world reveals flaws upon close enough scrutiny. It is to commit the logical fallacy of composition to assume that there must be attainment of perfection in the whole before there can be any attainment in the parts, attainment all the time before any time. It is important to recognize this, for one of the major foes of idealism is the defeatist attitude which, seeing obstacles which make the attainment of perfection impossible, relinquishes effort with a shrug of the shoulders and a "What's the use?"

3. IDEALS AS ILLUSIONS

Ideals are often stigmatized as "mere illusions." This view I should like as staunchly as possible to repudiate.

Some are and some are not "flights of fancy" in a moral sense. There are a real patriotism and a bogus patriotism; a legitimate pacifism and a bastard pacifism; a high-minded use of coercive force and a brutal violence which parades under its semblance. It is as important to the moral life to distinguish which ideals to follow as to follow the right ones when they are discerned. Of the criteria by which to judge ideals we shall say something later.[1]

The point which needs most to be made clear here is that it is improper to identify three concepts which are related but by no means identical: namely, *the cosmic reality of ideals,* their *moral validity,* and their *psychological reality.* Whether or not human ideals have cosmic status is a question which will be discussed when we consider the problem of God. The moral validity of ideals —that is, the question of which should and which should not be followed—is one which must not be overlooked. But before either of these questions can be respectfully considered it must be admitted that ideals really exist, and do something in life which is of great importance. If a person believes that "there is no reason to suppose that his own life has any more meaning than the life of the humblest insect that crawls from one annihilation to another,"[2] there is no sense in talking about ideals as regulative value-judgments. I shall not labor this point, for it is doubtful whether any one who holds this view will have read thus far.

[1]Particularly in Chapter XV.
[2]Joseph Wood Krutch, *The Modern Temper,* p. 9.

Whatever else may be denied of them, ideals have at least psychological existence; and if they have this, they are in so far forth *facts*. It is a naïvely materialistic assumption to hold that something which operates with potency to redirect life into different channels is any less "real" than a lump of physical matter.

4. THE RELATION OF MORAL TO OTHER IDEALS

When I said that every ideal has a volitional as well as a cognitive and emotional aspect, I said by implication that all ideals have an ethical element. I believe this to be true and important, though I recognize it to be a debatable statement. It is important because, if true, it indicates that man's moral quest permeates every attempt to escape not only from his sin but from his finitude.

Moral ideals are not the only type there is, but every ideal, whether of good craftsmanship, beauty, or intellectual achievement, has a moral foundation. An ideal is a concept of what ought to be, and "ought" is a moral term. This does not mean that an artist need necessarily conform to the accepted social code in his behavior in order to have high ideals of art. He may be as Bohemian as he likes, and unless he drinks himself into a state of physical or psychical abnormality he may still be a good artist. So too the scholar, whose ideals of painstaking pursuit and presentation of the truth are not dependent on the way he treats his wife. But no true artist *would try to be an artist* unless he felt the impulsion of an ideal of creativity, nor would the scientist be a scientist at all unless the ideal of a truth to be discovered had laid hold upon him. In either case, it is as if something objective had placed upon him the demand that the work be done. Lacking this impulsion, the work is neither art nor science, but pot-boiling.

5. ORIGINS OF THE MORAL IMPERATIVE

We have said that every human being is tainted with original sin and born into a state of finitude. He has also redeeming elements of original goodness, and from his sin and finitude he is in a measure saved through ideals.

We have just finished saying that these ideals, whether directly of an ethical nature or with an ethical impulsion to the pursuit of some non-moral value, seem to the person impelled by them to have an objective force. They are in us, yet from beyond us. It would be possible to move at once to the conclusion that they are from God. However, this conclusion, if we draw it, belongs further along in the argument. When a generation has largely lost its faith in idealism of any sort, the human validity of ideals has to be re-established before we can move to a faith in their cosmic foundations.

What is the source of this moral imperative? One way to account for it is to trace it to a combination of biological tendencies with social conditionings in the earlier, more impressionable years, and assume that this tells the whole story. I once had a discussion with a fellow-professor who urged in all seriousness that the heroism displayed in battle is wholly a product of "beef-steak and spankings," and that gratitude is simply the act of "one cat licking off another." In more famous words, Thomas

Hobbes many years ago characterized gratitude as a lively sense of favors yet to come,[3] and described the life of man upon earth as "solitary, poore, nasty, brutish, and short."[4]

Since the day of Hobbes there have been all sorts of attempts to reduce man to a biological organism, essentially one with the animal world though with a more complex nervous system which makes possible a greater rapidity, relevance, and retentiveness of responses in the conditioning process. There are many today who both believe and teach that moral ideals are merely complex conditionings of a psycho-physical animal organism. By so teaching they contribute to the dissolution of ideals; for the person who thinks of himself as a complex agglomeration of atoms or protoplasm—and nothing more than this—is not likely to put much trust in spiritual forces either within him or without. With apologies to Shakespeare for distorting his words from their context, "cool it with a baboon's blood" is an effective way to chill idealism and brew a materialistic spell. This does not mean that the person who believes a purely physiological interpretation of human nature to be the true one should refrain from saying so; but it is fair to ask that it should not be put forth with flippancy and a careless disregard of consequences.

There is much to be learned from the physiological psychologist about the processes by which ideals become operative in human experience. Some are acquired

[3]*Leviathan*, Chap. XV. "As Justice dependeth on Antecedent Covenant; so does Gratitude depend on Antecedent Grace. . . . For no man giveth, but with intention of Good to himselfe."
[4]*Ibid.*, Chap. XIII.

through rewards and punishments in which bodily as well as mental factors are involved. Probably all, in a sense, have relation to past experiences of pleasure and pain in which the body is the medium by which the feeling is aroused. Ideals arise not only through overt physical conditioning but through the process of introjection —the imaginative identification of one's personality with what is admired in another until the other person's standards are adopted as one's own. It is difficult to explain such identification wholly in physical terms.

The important thing, however, from the standpoint of a social philosophy is not these processes, but their interpretation. There is nothing devastating to religion or morals in any valid psychological knowledge of the processes by which consciences are moulded. What does become devastating is the mistaking of these processes for a total view, with the assumption that when we have learned how something happens we have learned that there is nothing in it.

In other words, it is the "fallacy of origins" rather than a knowledge of origins which is dangerous to idealism. To say that ideals are the product of biological and social forces is not to say that they are *merely* this, any more than to say that mountains are the product of the upheaval or erosion of the earth's crust is to deny them beauty and sublimity. Mountains objectively *are,* however they came to be in geological terms and whether or not there is a God in the universe. To know their geological history adds to their interest, to believe that "the firmament showeth His handiwork" may make it the more possible to lift one's eyes to the hills for strength. But lacking both types of knowledge one may still believe that mountains exist, and that human life in its æsthetic as well as economic aspects is different because of them. Similarly one may believe that ideals exist and that they have potency as forces redirecting human nature, whatever their psycho-physical or cosmic origins. To know the former adds understanding, to know the latter adds vitality to experience—but the experience itself is the indubitable datum.

To carry the figure farther, a mountain, as we experience it, is a combination of objective physical energy with a subjective apprehension and interpretation of sensory stimuli. It is both within and beyond us. So are ideals. They are within us, yet at least in their social and perhaps in their cosmic origins, they come to us from without. They operate subjectively, yet with objective power. It is this combination of objectivity with subjectivity that gives them potency for the moulding of life. Whatever their cosmic status, they are super-organic and super-individual; we accept or reject them at the "threshold of consent"; and by them we find direction.

Instead, then, of saying that ideals are merely the product of biological forces modified by social conditioning, it seems a more inclusive view to say that they are the product of an inherent tendency within man's nature which enables him to direct his life toward goodness and the mastery of limitations. The particular bent which any individual's ideals take—in brief, the kind of conscience he has—depends on hereditary and environmental forces, his past experience, and to some degree on his own reflection when confronted by situations of conflict. But *that he has ideals at all* is rooted in the fact that he is a human being. It is the capacity to rule his life by a non-coercive authority which pre-eminently sets him apart from the sub-human realm: it is this which empowers him to find inner salvation.

Chapter V

LEVELS OF IDEALISM

IT IS necessary now to survey the types of ideals by which men find salvation. They are not all on the same level, either as to potency or purity. It is probably apparent to the reader by this time that when I say "salvation" I refer not to a state of future life but to escape from the guilt and chaos which infests our temporal existence. I do not deny immortality, for there are reasons both philosophical and theological for holding it to be a legitimate faith.[1] However, our first concern is with salvation in the here and now.

Ideals might be classified in various ways, but I shall speak of three types in ascending levels. The criterion by which to judge one to be higher than another is their effectiveness in giving richness and balance to life.

I. PRUDENTIAL ADJUSTMENT

First, there is the ideal of prudential adjustment. "Safety first" might be taken as its motto. It has had a long history, ranging from the richness of the Greek "nothing in excess"[2] to much less attractive forms in the present

[1]I have stated some of these reasons in *Conflicts in Religious Thought*, Chap. XII.

[2]The Greeks had courage as one of the cardinal virtues. Except in its Epicurean strains, Greek ethics is not to be identified with prudential adjustment, but this seems to me to be in part a perverted form of the Greek spirit of moderation.

mores. In the report of the survey made by *Fortune* of the current attitudes of college students, there is an apt citation of the way it manifests itself:

The present-day college generation is fatalistic . . . the investigator is struck by the dominant and pervasive color of a generation that will not stick its neck out. It keeps its shirt on, . . . its chin up, and its mouth shut. If we take the mean average to be the truth, it is a cautious, subdued, unadventurous generation, unwilling to storm heaven, afraid to make a fool of itself, unable to dramatize its predicament. It may be likened to a very intelligent turtle, skeptical of its biological inheritance, the shell, but determined not to be a bull, a bear, or a goat. The turtle has security and . . .
Security is the summum bonum *of the present college* generation. . . . Yearners for security do not set foot on Everest or discover the Mountains of the Moon.[3]

There is no reason to decry such a quest for security as wholly bad. It is in part inevitable, certainly understandable. It involves concern not only for economic *terra firma* but for other legitimate values such as physical health and social approbation. All of these, at least under some circumstances, are much needed, and properly tempered with a sense of social responsibility, they are important assets to the smooth functioning of society. But what one feels the lack of here is the sense of social responsibility which drives heroes out of safe harbors into dangerous enterprises.

The idealism of caution is self-defeating. It is practical

[3] *Op. cit.,* "Youth in College," June, 1936. By permission of editors of *Fortune.*

only on a short-range view, for it fails either to present a spiritual breakwater against unavoidable storms, or to send one forth into the storms which must be stirred into being before our present society can be brought into anything like a state of safety for all.

2. SOCIALLY RESPECTED CHARACTER

A second level of idealism is that of socially respected character. It roots in respectability, but often goes beyond the bare minimum of conventional respectability. It displays itself in acts and attitudes of kindness, sympathy and generosity within the area of one's personal interest. It is the type of idealism which makes a person a good neighbor, an agreeable companion, an excellent husband and father, and a respected member of the community. There is in it an inseparable mixture of social conformity with genuine concern for others, and often, though not always, a considerable trace of religion. A person of this type of idealism usually feels no vital concern for persons or causes which lie beyond the circle of his own acquaintance or his own economic interests, but where he sees and knows what is at stake, he is willing to serve. This is the type of person who is well spoken of while he lives, and who gets a big attendance at his funeral when he dies.

This is as far as idealism goes with the majority of persons, and if we could be sure it would go thus far with all the people now living self-centered lives it would be an occasion for rejoicing. A community made up of such persons would be one in which there would be no lack of support for civic enterprises. Such persons are themselves, in most cases, the product of an excellent home training, often of a good education, and they want the next generation to have the best that can be had. Such persons are leaders in the Woman's Club, Parent-Teachers' Association, Masons and Eastern Star, Rotary and Kiwanis—sometimes in the church auxiliary and vestry.

I say "sometimes" because often they repudiate the religious matrix which has nourished them. Whether or not they are themselves the products of religious homes, they are the products of the civilizing, ameliorating influence of the Hebrew-Christian faith extending through many centuries. But failing to see the relevance of religion or the church to themselves, they often pass it by and live quite decent lives without it. To others whose outer conduct or inner self-control is little if at all different religion has some personal meaning, and they give the church at least nominal support.

This is the idealism of an ordinary "moral man" in an "immoral society." The fact that such morality often seems about equally attractive and admirable whether it is, or is not, consciously joined with religion makes a problem for many minds, and drives some into humanism. The question is no new one, for in the New England theocracy it was necessary to work out the curious Halfway Covenant to give political standing to those who were not converted but who lived as well as those who were.

The fact that one often cannot tell the difference, by his actions, between a decent Christian and a decent atheist is one of the most serious indictments against Christianity. It indicates, from one angle, how far religion has merely been sugar-coating for conventional standards. But the question has another side, less damning to Christian influence. The answer lies, first, in the grateful acceptance of any attractiveness of character, however it comes. There is nothing to be gained by trying to maintain that persons who are not consciously religious are in reality whited sepulchres full of dead men's bones. The second part of the answer lies in a recognition of the indirect influence of religion in the lives of those who now repudiate it; and a third in the awareness that there are greater heights of idealism than these to which nothing save the power of a religious dynamic will carry one.

3. TRIUMPHANT RELIGION

The third level of idealism is sometimes characterized as that in which life has been redeemed by divine grace. It would be convenient to make this distinction, but in honesty it seems to me necessary to say that some persons in the area just described have also been thus redeemed, and through divine grace have found personal sweetness and light. This third level might better be called the idealism of triumphant religion.

Its distinctive attribute is breadth of vision and depth of soul. It calls for more than conventional service within restricted areas of personal interest. As exemplars of it, I think of St. Francis among the poor, of Father Damien among the lepers, of Schweitzer in present-day Africa and Kagawa in Japan, of Howard Kester and Claude Williams, willing to risk lynching or suffer flogging for the share-croppers of Arkansas, of numerous brave souls of my acquaintance who are willing to risk public disapproval and endanger their economic security to proclaim ideals which they believe to be grounded in the Christian Gospel.

A roll of the heroes of triumphant religion, if one could be made, would have to include also those many persons in humbler ranks who perform serenely, triumphantly, creatively, the daily grind of humdrum tasks in home and church and community. Doing such works without complaint or self-pity, without personal aggrandizement and without bitterness under censure, they "live their religion." Such persons, as far as I have observed, are found only among those to whom religion is a vital, life-transforming power.

This third level of idealism is marked by a dynamic union of social vision and social passion, generated not merely out of conformity to community standards of respectability and service, but rooted in the depths of life. In such lives there is personal poise and mastery—the ability to rise above the tragic exigencies of life and to conquer the fear, loneliness and bewilderment which doth so easily beset us. In such there is, with personal serenity, an out-going quality of life which generates sympathy for all persons and courage to serve the needy, not simply at the cost of some personal inconvenience but at the cost of treading the *via dolorosa*.

On this level, the philosophy of "the other cheek" and "the second mile" becomes more than a bit of pious rhetoric. On this level the Christian valuation of personality and the Christian ideal of service become "second nature," a new nature superimposed by religion upon conventional altruism. No magical perfection of character eventuates, but there is here a "sanctification" of life in the sense of an often-unconscious achievement of saintly living.

This third level of idealism might, then, be termed the level of active saintliness. "Integration of personality" is another, but a much more barren, name for the same thing. Such persons never think of themselves as saints, but others judge them to be such. The quality of saintliness is difficult to describe, but easy to recognize in those rare individuals in whom one sees it manifest. Such lives have a winsomeness which attracts by its own compulsion. Such recognition of greatness in personality is the most effective answer to the charge that religion is mere useless form.

These are the levels on which we live. Superimposed upon a morass of guilt, fear, loneliness and bewilderment to bring order out of an otherwise chaotic life are certain powerful ideals. The idealism of calculating security, which dominates the greater number of people, keeps us relatively free of external assault but gives little support to the inner life. This is the level of Epicurean irresponsibility.

A lesser, but very considerable, number surmount this level to live on a plane in which are inextricably mingled egoism and altruism, the desire for social approval and a real, though limited, concern for the welfare of others. The motivation here is sometimes Epicurean, sometimes Stoic, sometimes Christian—often a vague mixture of all three. Life on this level, whether or not in touch with religion, is reasonably happy, reasonably successful, not very sacrificial and not genuinely triumphant. The lack of triumph in the deeper reaches is not revealed in ordinary smooth-going situations, but a sudden crisis betrays the lack of inner moorings. Fear, worry and anger, often jealousy and revenge, have their innings even though by dint of long discipline an outer composure is preserved. An emergency, like a fire or flood, a loss of money or even a sudden access of prosperity, sweeps one off his feet.

Only on the third level is there genuine stability, serenity, and the kind of service which goes beyond obvious claims, giving freely and seeking no reward. In the rare souls who attain this type of personality, there are wholeness of life and true saintliness.[4]

---

[4]There are no sharp lines of cleavage between these levels. They blend into each other. Few of us are "pure types." Yet there are distinguishable differences in the way people live which clearly correlate with differences in dominant ideals.

Chapter VI

AN APPROACH TO TRIUMPHANT
RELIGION

WE HAVE traced certain effects and causes of the dissolution of ideals and have indicated some basic characteristics of human nature which both necessitate and make possible the moulding of life by ideals. Our next task is to examine by what practical strategy and by what logical approach ideals of a vitalizing, life-transforming nature can be made operative.

I. TRIUMPHANT RELIGION AS A NORM

If what was said in the last chapter is a true description of the levels of idealism on which men live, it is apparent that the third ought to become normative for all who live on lower levels. Only here do we find personality which is genuinely triumphant over sin and chaos—triumphant not in the sense of complete freedom from these limitations, but triumphant in the power to live with an active saintliness of character and a serenity undaunted by annoyance or adversity.

Not all persons will agree that this third level is a desirable objective. Saintliness and serenity are apt to suggest too much of quiescence; while to those who place a high estimate upon tranquillity, service of unpopular causes is an unwelcome challenge to a strenuousness thought to be antithetical to "the spiritual life." Saintliness involves not mere passive resistance to "the slings and arrows of outrageous fortune," but an active going out to meet them —even an activity which sets them stirring when they might otherwise lie unstirred. Because of this paradoxical demand the third level is more apt to be admired from afar than accepted as regulative for actual living.

Religious thought may be priestly, or it may be prophetic, but it is seldom both. The distinction is imbedded deep in the history of religion. The priest promises security—at least inner security and often external security as well through observance of the obligations of worship; the prophet challenges this as blasphemy unless joined to active effort for human good. Priests we have always with us, like the poor. Prophets are much rarer, and when priests get too unbearably complacent about the poor, prophets emerge to denounce a way of living which lets some men be exploited for others' gain. History has not bred many saints, but where they have appeared, they have most often united in one person the prophetic and priestly functions.

Mary and Martha both have their followers; faith and works their champions. The view I have suggested emphasizes the necessity of the integrated union, in one personality, of faith with works, of personal power and social passion. A religious leader must be both priest and prophet if he would be truly effective. If one says that this is impossible, the most telling answer is the citation of living personalities who actually achieve this union, and who through it live creative and triumphant lives.

We are speaking now of levels of achievement which lie frankly beyond the aspiration of most people. The second level, that of decent, socially respected character, is all the many want, or see any need of having. Many are satisfied in practice with the first but not usually in theory. So powerful is the impulse to self-preservation that in a concrete situation the majority of persons, whether young or old, will cast aside self-respect and even society's respect to save their skins. The contemporary fading out of the concept of sin has left many young arguers ready to contend that the only harm in any act lies in getting caught. Yet few of them really believe this. The kind of people they admire, and rather implicitly expect to become, are the conventionally respectable and highly respected members of the community whom we have described under the second category. Saintliness, so labelled, does not appeal to them except with the casual interest one might have in a museum-piece. Personally, they have no intention of becoming saints, apostles, prophets, or martyrs; and the idea of dying for causes, even close-at-hand causes, does not greatly interest them.[1]

This situation tempts one to feel that if the environing atmosphere can be pulled up to the second level or somewhere near it, that is as far in most cases as we can expect to get.

[1]Recently after a discussion at a student conference on campus morals, a student asked me what could be done about cheating on her campus. When I suggested that students might take some responsibility for inducing offenders to report themselves, she replied, "But if you do, you'll be unpopular!" When I remarked that most moral enterprises introduce the danger of unpopularity and that this might have something to do with the meaning of the cross, her straightforward observation was, "We don't want to go to the cross; we want to be popular!" Against such honest egocentricity there is no arguing.

Yet if a creative idealism is to be generated in our day, to the strengthening of personal character and the saving of society from chaos, it is necessary to aim farther. Reformers have to be bred. Social vision and social passion have to be generated, and imbedded in something that will hold under strain. If ideas do not become ideals, dynamically propulsive toward a more just and more friendly world, then is most of our teaching in vain. The educative process becomes merely the sounding brass of the college band, or the tinkling cymbals of chimes in the library tower, if teachers do not somehow challenge students to the idealism of triumphant living.

Few, if any, wiser men than Plato have ever lived. It was Plato who said, placing the words in the mouth of Socrates:

Some things I have said of which I am not altogether confident. But that we shall be better and braver and less helpless if we think that we ought to inquire, than we should have been if we indulged in the idle fancy that there was no knowing and no use in seeking to know what we do not know;—that is a theme upon which I am ready to fight in word and deed, to the utmost of my power.[2]

Similarly, whatever the doubts and uncertainties that beset current thinking, it may be affirmed resolutely, and fought for, that we shall be better and braver and less helpless if we have an idealism that is rooted both in ideas and action.

[2]*Meno*, 86.

2. A DOUBLE APPROACH

There are two ways of achieving creative idealism, not mutually exclusive but for their full effectiveness conjoined. These are the ways of incarnation in life and of the clarification of ideas. They correspond to the emotional and the cognitive elements in an ideal. An idea is not an ideal unless it grips the emotions to the point of becoming dynamic, but neither is an emotional impulse an ideal unless it has some content of idea. It takes both the manifestation of ideals in personal living and a theoretical acceptance of intellectual foundations to make an ideal become mandatory for character. Whether as adults or children, we grow to be like the people we admire; but if we are thinking persons, we have to be sure our heroes are not self-deceived.

If feeling is either weak or misdirected, if ideas are either nebulous or false, ideals become correspondingly vapid or dangerous. To illustrate, a purely educational, non-propagandist approach to the establishment of world peace through a knowledge of international relations is based on true ideas inadequately galvanized. Such education is to be steadily promoted for its long-range values, but not relied upon in an emergency. On the other hand, an emotionally grounded pacifism which lacks adequate knowledge of what makes wars and what must be done to get rid of them is politically futile and tapers off into an empty sentimentality. As examples of powerful ideals which I believe to be dangerous because emotionally accepted with great vitality on the basis of false ideas might be cited the loyalty of the German youth to Hitler; or the loyalty of most Americans to the capitalistic system. If you, my reader, feel your indignation rising that I should thus assume either of these to be in error, you substantiate my point; for your feeling and mine must be tested by the conformity of idea to empirical fact before either of us will have a true ideal— that is, will have more than an emotional impulse on which to base opinion. (I could upon occasion cite some facts on which I base my ideas—and therefore my ideals—about both Hitler and the capitalistic system, but to do so would carry us off the main track of discussion.)[3]

If this point is accepted—that an ideal to be constructive must have both a pure and intense emotional dynamic and an empirically grounded, logically satisfying basis of idea, the application to the inculcation of triumphant religion is obvious. Religious leaders need to incarnate in their own lives that which they believe to be of supreme worth, and need equally to get a clear, defensible conviction of the truth of basic religious ideas. Neither process is easy. Still more difficult is it to achieve both at once. Yet both are imperative if we are to arrive anywhere. With such a chart we know where we are going; and to know both what we are steering toward and by what route to travel is worth much, even though in the way are many bogs and bumps.

The basic root of much of the ineptitude in current living, current teaching, current preaching is to be found in a splitting apart of that which ought to be in union. Religion, though of too many types to speak of in generalities,

---

[3]Chapter V of *The Resources of Religion* states some observations upon this point.

has on the whole been more concerned with personal piety than with ideas; and where ideas have got the upper hand, as in most forms of religious liberalism, sin and redemption have been genteelly, but not too politely, bowed out the door. Secular instruction has been primarily concerned with the ingestion of facts and whetting of instruments of thought; and where the bearing of such facts and thought processes have had any relevance to personal living it has been assumed that intellectual culture would save society. The result is a disintegration of the meaningfulness of existence to the point where there is not much left to fight for. Yet because there are some who not only keep fighting but live triumphantly, it is possible to believe that "we shall be better and braver and less helpless" if we examine how they do it.

3. INCARNATION IN LIFE

Saintliness, like any other object of beauty, attracts by its own drawing power when it is recognized. If it does not attract at least the elect few whose eyes are undimmed by the glare of campus foot-lights, there is something unsaintly about it. Or to vary the term, since most of us would feel embarrassed to be called saints, wholeness and richness of life are their own best argument for religious foundations. It is a common saying that good religion, like good music, needs not argument but rendition.

I shall not try to tell in much detail *how* to incarnate religion in life.[4] There are no specific rules by which it can be taught, and while there are techniques about it, it

[4] Cf. *ibid.*, Chap. VIII, for further discussion of this subject.

72

comes mainly by vision and depth of experience. "He that hath ears to hear"—and eyes to see—will discover; and to try to give advice would be presumptuous, if not futile. Yet there are some things to do and not to do, and it may not be out of place to mention some pointers and some pitfalls.

First among the pointers is the matter of prayer. The intellectual problems centering in prayer belong subsequent to a discussion of the idea of God. It is with its practical and moral aspects that I am here concerned, though these are largely contingent on an acceptance of its theoretical justification. I mention it first because it is the most vital element in the generation of creative idealism.

Prayer is essentially a process by which ideals are enabled to become operative in our lives. It may be more than this, but it is at least this. We said, in analyzing the nature of ideals, that they have both a subjective and an objective aspect; they are within us, yet seem to command from beyond us. Prayer opens the subjective receptors in personality to the directing and vitalizing power of that which lays demands upon us for the purification of life. Prayer does not, at least in most cases, directly impart ideas, but it clears away obstacles to straight thinking; it does not implant emotions which have had no previous stimulation, but it enables one to choose between competing emotions and to act with power upon those chosen as worthy. To illustrate from a simple problem which often interests students, prayer will not enable one to pass an examination by giving knowledge to the lazy, but it will enable one to think with clarity about the knowledge already acquired; it will not keep a person from cheating who has never been taught to be honest, but it will strengthen one's moral reserves under temptation.

If prayer can thus clarify and motivate ideals, it does the most important thing that could be done. If any one wishes to say that its effect is from the subconscious rather than God, I should quarrel only with the "rather than," for there is no reason why God should not work through the subconscious as well as through any other channel. Freud has peopled the subconscious with strange demons, but it is possible that God placed there some angels of light before Freud appeared on the scene.

The method of prayer follows from its nature. There are many ways to pray, but the prime necessity is to combine passivity with activity. To have too much of either is to nullify its value. The more extreme forms of mysticism surrender self-direction in the attempt to be receptive; while with most Christians prayer is largely perfunctory because of lack of receptivity. The objective side of our idealism needs a chance to operate within us, but the subjective side needs to be open to receive whatever of power or light may be given.

A second pointer toward the incarnation of triumphant religion in life is the redemptive power of suffering. The problem of pain, like that of prayer, has deep and complicated intellectual ramifications, some of which will be discussed in a later chapter.[5] I do not believe all suffering to be punitive, and I do not believe it to be entirely the

[5]Chapter XIII.

will of God. The significant fact, however, is that there is no suffering of a normal personality which has not the possibility of being turned into channels of power. I say "normal personality" because in some stages of psychic distintegration there are limits beyond which the creative forces of neither man nor God are apparently able to go. In *dementia praecox* or Mongolian idiocy, there is no use of talking about the redemptive power of pain within the person thus afflicted. But it is not of these I am speaking; it is of those close enough to "normalcy" to be able to regulate their lives in ordinary matters. If these crumple instead of growing triumphant under strain, it is because there is something either wrong or lacking in their ideals. A friend who had first-hand experience with the destructive floods of 1935 told me the people acted like the furniture; those firmly constructed stood up under the strain, while others went to pieces like the tables and chairs put together with glue.

The analogy fails, however, at an important point, for no article of furniture is the stronger for the deluge. Ideals are the growing point of character, and there are few, if any, truly triumphant personalities who have not been lifted through strain. To the outward observer, such serenity may show no trace of struggle, but pain has spoken inwardly its tidings of redemption and release. These lives suggest its alchemy:

> She drew off her life's bitter brew—
> Heartache, failure, disaster—
> And, by a chemistry she knew,
> Distilled it into laughter.

Each night she yielded God her soul . . .
Emptied, earthy and dim;
Each dawn he gave her a golden bowl
Bubbling over the brim.

All who tasted were vivified
By the utter joy she offered,
But one, with solemn visage, sighed
"She's probably never suffered."[6]

There are other channels which lead toward the incarnation of triumphant religion in life. Among these are religious education, when it does not lose its content in absorption with techniques; evangelism, when it is not hysterical and æsthetically repulsive; devotional study of the Bible and other great classics of the soul, when such study does not become mechanical and perfunctory; discussion, when the give-and-take of ideas does not degenerate into a contest of wits; biography, when the tale is not over-told. The most effective channels, however, reduce to two. These are day by day contacts with living, breathing persons in whom the spirit of man is manifestly the candle of the Lord; and direct personal participation in the struggle to bring society into closer conformity to the ideal of the kingdom of God. Without these two, the rest will be largely in vain. This suggests without further elaboration how important it is to have the right personalities in a school faculty; and how vital it is that students be set to doing something besides ingesting

[6]"The Merrymaker," by Woodbridge O. Johnson, Jr. In *The Christian Century*, August 7, 1935. Used by permission.

theoretical knowledge and pouring it out again upon the scrawled pages of examination blue-books.

I said I should also mention a few pitfalls. I do this with trepidation, since evil spirits are legion, and there is no such uniformity in besetting sins as in avenues to conquest. I shall mention "seven devils," each the inverted form of a virtue, which are the most insidious temptations of high-minded persons. These are dominance, proceeding from a legitimate self-confidence; quiescence, generated out of the temperament of philosophic objectivity; intolerance, born of an intense conviction that one's own views are right; irresponsibility in small matters, born of the faith that one has a great work to do; irritability, emerging out of nervous tension and overwork; excessive self-condemnation, which arises to torment the sensitive conscience not held in even keel by a sense of proportion; and finally, the secret yearning for applause, which perhaps as Milton suggested is "the last infirmity of noble minds." If one can sweep out these devils and not leave an empty house to which they can return, his soul becomes a hostel on the highroad to triumphant living.

Thus far we are brought in a survey of the task of incarnating in life the goals set up by a vision of triumphant religion. This is not all there is to be said. The great religious personalities of all ages have left their witness as signposts pointing others along the road to achievement. But it is a road which each must travel for himself; and until he has traveled it—or tried to travel it—he is likely not to understand the directions.

Chapter VII

AN APPROACH TO PROBLEMS
OF KNOWLEDGE

THE APPROACH to triumphant living, we said, involved
both incarnation in life and the clarification of ideas. A
study of the latter will carry us out of the field of social
philosophy with which we have thus far mainly dealt,
and into the province of the philosophy of religion. But
it will first be necessary to examine the nature and
criteria of religious knowledge.

I. WHAT KNOWLEDGE IS OF MOST WORTH?

For epistemology, as it ordinarily dominates philosophical discussion, I have less respect than most philosophers. It is possible "always to be whetting the sword
and never using it," and the discussions of theory of
knowledge to which I am accustomed to listen at philosophical gatherings seem to me to have, in most cases,
little relevance to human living or to the understanding
of the universe. Metaphysics is not all there is of philosophy, but whenever one stops short of metaphysics he fails
to fulfil the philosophic function of being "the spectator
of all time and all existence." Epistemology is valuable in
the degree to which it enables one with intellectual as-

surance to formulate a unified world-view. Taken as an end of inquiry in itself, it becomes a substitute for philosophy.

I am not a pragmatist; yet I believe the pragmatists have contributed a principle which is of great value in determining the proper ends of philosophical inquiry. If an idea *makes a difference* it is worth pursuing; if not, one might better direct attention elsewhere. This "difference" need not be taken in too narrowly instrumentalist a sense, for quite apart from any practical application, the truth in pure science or pure mathematics is worth pursuing for the sake of the difference there is between knowledge and ignorance.

There is necessarily an element of subjective judgment in every person's estimate as to what truth is worth pursuing. This contributes both to the chaos and to the infinite variety of systems of thought and is a wholesome corrective to intellectual complacency. Both the scientist and the theologian, in pursuit of what *is,* need the philosopher as a gad-fly to remind them constantly that something else *may be* because of other aspects of reality not taken into account.

Every philosopher, seeking to interpret an infinitely complex world, chooses from it the elements which seem to him to be of most worth as principles by which to organize the rest of it. Thus every system in some sense begs the question. But lest the foes of philosophy turn this admission against its enterprise, I hasten to say that there is no other intellectual or practical pursuit which does not do likewise. The scientist is a scientist because

79

he believes his way of finding truth to be the best way and his object of search the most important object. The artist does the same about the apprehension and expression of beauty, the mystic about "the practice of the presence of God." The analogy can be carried on a less spiritual plane into politics and business, golf and contract bridge. Except as one is coerced by economic, political or physical necessity, nobody pursues for long what does not seem to him at the time to be worth pursuing.

The relevance of this to the problem of this book is twofold. We have already suggested that the present state of psychic and social disintegration arises from a decline in the sense that there is something worth while to pursue; in short, from the loss of a faith. The other point of relevance is that in the creation of the intellectual framework of a faith, the practical demands of living—that is, the question of "what makes a difference"—must be taken into account with open eyes and not with judgment clouded by subtle processes of rationalization. To revert to the statement made above that every intellectual system begs its question, it is one thing to do this and know that one is doing it, and quite another to be self-deceived into thinking that here at last is truth wholly free from subjective interest.

My philosophy is based frankly on the assumption that morals and religion are man's most important interests. I believe this to be true because life itself is more inescapable than anything else save death, and morals and religion make a supreme difference in living. There is nothing more important than the questions of the standards by which to live in our inevitable living and the supports, if any, by which to be sustained in the innermost areas of personality.

To morals and religion as life's most important interests might be added art. The soul is limited and in a sense "damned" which through lack of vision, or barriers to beholding it, is constrained to live without a sense of beauty. Yet the æsthetic is less primary than the ethical or religious life of man because its social consequences are less far-reaching. No one ought to be obliged to live in ugliness; but ugliness is less corrupting to personality than is an atmosphere of moral sordidness or gross irreverence.

It may readily and legitimately be asked whether morals and religion are more important than science. Fortunately, we are not obliged to choose one to the exclusion of the other. Yet one's procedure in the search for truth centers in, and takes its departure from, the question as to whether fact or value is the more important. In this sense there is an eternal conflict, not to be reconciled by any liberal synthesis, between science and religion. Science seeks facts and is only secondarily concerned with their relevance to life; religion seeks the enrichment of life and is secondarily concerned with the gathering of factual data. Such a divergence goes far deeper than any question of the historicity of Genesis, and remains after liberal theology has broken down all inhibitions against giving natural explanations of the miracles.

Scientific fact—in so far as it is really *fact* and not

dogmatic assumption—is not to be rejected as either untrue or unimportant. To know the truth is an essential approach to freedom. One can go a long way before science and religion part company, and they must be synthesized before being separated. Yet when confronted with the question as to whether it is more important to know impersonally what can be objectively verified, or to make judgments both from these factual data and from intuitive insights as to how life ought to be lived, one has to make a choice.

The general tenor of one's philosophy will depend on the choice he makes. The viewpoint from which this book is written is that "life is more than logic" and more than factual data, though both logical coherence and factual data must have a place—and a large place—if life is to be lived at its fullest and best.

2. A DILEMMA, AND WAYS OF ESCAPE

If morals and religion be accepted as the two most important human interests, we are immediately in a dilemma. The paradox confronts us that these are also the two areas in which it is least possible to have objective canons, and therefore, the two fields in which there is least social agreement. Where we need standards most, we seem to have them least. For the resolution of this dilemma several courses may be followed.

One is the position of religious and moral skepticism. The skeptic holds that since no objective, verifiable knowledge is attainable in these fields, such knowledge is not worth pursuing. The religious skeptic usually gives up

both the pursuit and the experience of religion; in moral
skepticism the demands of living make this impossible
and one commonly lives by the conventional standards
in which he was reared while maintaining theoretically
that "there is nothing either good or bad but thinking
makes it so." Such ethical relativism is very widespread
both in academic and popular circles.

The second way is the position of religious humanism.
The humanist denies the availability of knowledge of
God, and with it the reality of God; but he retains as an
ethical norm the supreme value of personality. From this
he constructs his ideal of social justice, and labors for a
world in which all personalities shall have an opportunity
to live richly.

The third way is that of Professor Wieman and other
so-called "empirical theists." These have a high sense of
the importance of religion and of the need of grounding
it on dependable foundations; they have also a high regard for the methods of the natural sciences. As a result
they establish both religion and morals on an empirical
basis, and attempt to eliminate all supernatural elements.
The result is an idea of God which is concentrated rather
than diffuse; that is, limited in scope and perhaps in potency, but less subject to the charge of wishful thinking
than the orthodox concept of a personal, supernatural
deity. Such theists have, in general, an empirical theory
of morals as well as religion.

A fourth way of resolving the paradox is found in various types of supernaturalism—authoritarian, intuitive,
æsthetic, or cosmological. In spite of the lines of demarca-

tion drawn by Professors Wieman and Meland in *American Philosophies of Religion* I believe that most of these distinctions are differences in emphasis rather than type. Supernaturalists do, however, vary significantly in their judgment of the degree of certainty with which God may be known. All supernaturalists believe that there is more in the universe than the natural order of things can reveal to us with verifiable certainty. Many supernaturalists believe that we have dependable knowledge of a more-than-human deity through one channel or another, or a combination of many channels; but that knowledge falls short of absolute certainty. The authoritarian or mystical supernaturalist holds that we do have such certainty, but that this comes through revelation rather than through the method of the sciences. Also, in their estimate of the foundations of morality supernaturalists vary widely, running the gamut from a spontaneous assumption that anything written in the Bible or emerging from raw intuition represents the will of God to the position that all morality is empirically grounded and independent of a religious framework.

3. PRACTICAL AND ABSOLUTE CERTAINTY

In speaking of certainty, it is necessary to distinguish between *practical certainty* and *absolute certainty*. We have practical certainty of many things, and these we are justified in saying we know; yet we have absolute certainty of very few.

When Descartes set out to doubt everything which could be doubted, he was left with his own consciousness of doubt as the only thing indubitably certain. While most of Descartes' inferences from this seem to me to be wrong, I believe he was right in making the content of an individual's own mind the only datum of which that individual can be immediately certain. I know what I am thinking; I do not know "beyond the shadow of a doubt" whether what I am thinking corresponds with reality. There is always the possibility that what I seem now to be experiencing as reality is the experience of an hallucination or a dream, that what I seem to recall clearly has suffered the vitiation of memory. As Santayana has put it in famous words, without "animal faith" we are reduced to "the solipsism of the present moment." Tennyson expressed the same idea in poetry when he said:

> Thou canst not prove that I who speak with thee
> Am not thyself in converse with thyself.

Yet it is obvious that we do not go around saying, "I think I am one person and you another, but I may be talking to myself; I think I am standing on the floor but maybe I am climbing a tree; I think I ate a poached egg for breakfast, but perhaps I only dreamed I did!" Although some latitude may be allowed absent-minded professors in such matters, even they would soon be in institutions as inmates rather than instructors if they kept this up very long. What we do, if we have our wits, is to regulate our lives on the practical certainty—that is, on the faith which converges with knowledge—that there are other people around us, that we exist in a world of physical nature, that with due caution we may trust our mental powers to give us at least part of the truth about the world.

Carneades was right when he said, "Probability is the guide of life." When young debaters, having marshalled their arguments, end with a grandiloquent "I have proved—," my philosophical sensibilities wince. One may say legitimately that he has proved the formal consistency of a set of mathematical relations, and a Q. E. D. has a rightful place in geometry that it does not have in argument. One may also say that he has proved the formal consistency of a set of logical propositions; but since the premises of a syllogism may be untrue, the validity of a conclusion gives no assurance of the truth of that conclusion.

Of the immediate content of conscious experience and of the consistency of mathematical and logical relations we may assert a degree of absoluteness not permissible elsewhere. But this does not mean we are shut up to universal skepticism in other fields. We have a practical certainty of many things, and manage to live by these assumptions with a fair measure of success. To illustrate, I do not have to prove that my food is germ-proof before I eat it; I act on the comfortable assumption that unless there is some reason to think otherwise, I can eat it and it will nourish me. This *practical* certainty may also be a *provisional* certainty, for if there is any need to know more exactly, I can find out from the experts its approximate bacterial content. But if before eating I were to wait for indubitable certainty, the chances are that I should starve to death while waiting.

God is one of many concepts of which we must say, "I believe" rather than, "I have proved." Yet this limitation is no calamity. To demand certainty where we cannot have it is to undercut moral endeavor; to claim to have it where we do not is to undercut intellectual integrity. Only if the universe and our minds were put together otherwise than they are could we expect to have absolute certainty in all fields of knowledge. We might better be honestly satisfied with the knowledge we can have than to yearn for, or claim to have attained, what cannot be ours.

Yet with a frank recognition of these limitations, it still remains true that there are *degrees* of certainty. We are more sure of the existence of human beings than of God, of the physical world than of immortality, of 90° angles in a building than of the honesty of the carpenter who constructs them. These differences in degrees of certainty are as important as is the fact that there is an element of assumption involved in most of the things we claim to know.

We noted above that the most important areas of life, religion and morals, are those in which we have least of the kind of certainty which takes shape as social agreement. For this there is a reason. Religion and morals involve judgments of value, and whatever we may believe about the objectivity of values in a metaphysical sense, there is always in any value judgment a core of subjectivity. Nothing would be a value unless it were a value to *somebody,* and the many "somebodies" that make up the world prize many different things. Objectively, also, there is a ground for variability in the fact that religion and morals relate to the whole of our many-sided life. Were their scope more limited, they could be confined more neatly.

But if we cannot have the certainty—or relative certainty—of social agreement,[1] we must find our practical certainty elsewhere. What we can know we ought to try to know, leaving the door open for such corrections as may come from further sight or insight and granting to others the right to hold their opinions in so far as these are the product of intelligent search.

In the next chapter it will be necessary to consider by what procedure we can best find such certainty as it is possible to find in the field of religious knowledge. In so doing we shall have to be careful not to confuse fact and value, running into the assumption that what ought to be, is. But we shall need to be equally on guard against the assumption that the road of empirical science is the only road which leads to truth. Moral and religious values do more than furnish an incentive to seek truth. They do this, but they furnish also some of the data by which to find it.

---

[1] I use the term "social agreement" rather than "objective verifiability" because the latter is a question-begging term. Its use assumes that everything ought to be subjected to the methods appropriate in the physical sciences. It is by no means certain that this is the only way to arrive at knowledge.

Chapter VIII

SYNOPTIC SUPERNATURALISM

AN EMPIRICAL examination of the facts of existence obviously involves a value judgment at least at the beginning and end of the process. One would not make such an examination unless he thought it to be worth making; having made it, he would condemn it as so much wasted effort unless from it could be drawn a conclusion which would be worth something to somebody. This principle holds, whether in practical achievement or the search for truth.

The relevance of this relation of value to discovery, and in particular to the discovery of factual knowledge, I have tried to suggest in the preceding chapter. A survey of life in its totality—in so far as a finite human being can see life as a whole—suggests that morals and religion are the most important aspects of existence because they relate most intimately to all we inevitably must experience. Confronted by the dilemma presented by the situation that in these most important areas we have least certain knowledge, we were led to canvass some ways of escape. It was observed that supernaturalists, though agreeing as to the impossibility of limiting knowledge to that which can be objectively verified in the physical order of nature, are nevertheless not in agreement as to the degree of certainty attainable through other channels. This made necessary a re-examination of what is meant by certainty, with the conclusion that though practical certainty may legitimately be termed knowledge, it is not to be identified with absolute certainty. The latter, taken in a strict sense, is not to be found outside of the immediate data of consciousness and the formal consistency of mathematical and logical relations. If the latter type is not to be had in science, its absence is not to be mourned in religion, though it is necessary to recognize *degrees* of certainty and seek for as much as possible in any field investigated.

I. SOME DEFINITIONS OF TERMS

We are ready now to see more specifically what this means when applied to religion. The type of epistemological approach by which I believe we can best arrive at dependable religious knowledge I shall call a *synoptic supernaturalism*. The term is chosen with the awareness that both parts of it are easily subject to misunderstanding. I must begin, therefore, by trying to make clear what I mean.

Synoptic means "seeing together." By the word synoptic I do not mean to suggest anything in the nature of a summary or short-cut, like the synopsis of a continued story in a magazine. Rather, synopsis in its philosophical sense is quite the reverse, and implies the principle of inclusiveness. The synoptic vision is that which sees things from all angles in a related whole. Whether the description of what is thus seen is stated in a paragraph or in a five-foot shelf of volumes is irrelevant, though the chances are against any true synopsis in a view so cluttered with detail that it takes a vast deal of verbiage to describe it. The synoptic view, when one really achieves it, is simple —but not with the simplicity of the simple-minded who fail to see complexity. The simplicity which is won through taking pains to see everything discernible is a long way removed from the pseudo-simplicity of failing to discover that there is anything to see.

Supernatural means "above the natural." In adopting this dangerous word—the storm-center of much theological discussion in these days—I do not mean to affirm any abrupt cleavage of the natural from the supernatural. The supernatural does not rest on top of the natural like the upper story of a house with a ceiling between. Still less is it somewhere up in the sky where "visibility unlimited" makes what lies within and beyond it invisible. And still less does it mean something spookish, as if disembodied spirits might be roaming around among us.[1] All these connotations supernaturalism has had, and because it has had them it has gone out of favor with realistically-minded people. But it is a good word badly misused, and because it expresses more exactly than any other a great idea which I believe to be a true one, I should like to try to help restore it to favor.

The supernatural, as the "more than natural," does not connote a separate realm of being, but an aspect of the

---

[1]When I told a friend that I was going to lecture on "synoptic supernaturalism," she looked bewildered and made no observation about the first term, but of the second remarked, "I thought people who went to college didn't believe in ghosts and witches any more."

world of existence which permeates and gives meaning to all existence. To assert belief in the supernatural is not to assert discontinuity but the most intimate kind of continuity with the world in which we all must live. The supernatural is not identical with the natural, for supernature is the ultimate source of existence and the goal of values which gives meaning to nature. Though it is not identical with the natural, neither is it severed from it.

This can perhaps be illustrated by an analogy. The knack of walking depends on the ability to keep one foot on the ground while the other is off. No child could learn to walk who did not discover this trick. To keep both feet on the ground is either to stand still or be dragged; to try to keep both feet off the ground is to be successful only in a leap or a hop which cannot last long. There is a situation here by which to understand the relation of the natural to the supernatural, if we do not push the analogy too far. The supernatural is not a separate world to leap off to; it is that in integrated union with the natural which allows us to go forward toward ends achievable only by such union. Anybody who would find its meaning, either practically or in speculation, must "keep one foot on the ground." But not both. To keep both feet on the ground is to be a naturalist; to take both off is to be a transcendentalist, an extreme mystic, or an authoritarian dogmatist. What we are looking for is a method by which to have progressive certainty and progressive moral achievement.

To use less figurative terms, our knowledge of the natural order of things is essential but not complete. If one sets out to try to explain either man or the cosmos in purely naturalistic terms, he leaves out the most important aspects. Origins, purpose, destiny—all require something "above the natural" for an understanding of what is natural. What this means more concretely we shall attempt to discover in the remainder of the book.

2. ELEMENTS IN THE SYNOPTIC APPROACH

By the synoptic approach I mean that authority, intuition—whether ethical, æsthetic or mystical, the pragmatic test in individual and social living, the evidence of the natural sciences, and the demands of logical consistency, not only *do have* but *ought to have* their place in enabling us to formulate our idea of God and related concepts. This does not mean that any idea we get from any of these channels may be held along with any other. I am not advocating a philosophy of higgledy-piggledy. Were one to rely on the method of authority, unpurged, he would certainly not be able to rely with equal assurance on the method of the physical sciences. For example, one cannot at the same time believe that God created the earth in six days and rested on the seventh, and that creation is a process which it has taken geological aeons to bring to its present state. But fortunately, one does not have to find himself in this predicament if his use both of authority and of scientific method is truly synoptic.

What I am suggesting is not merely an eclectic but a coherently unified view, an approach in which the defects of each method find a corrective in a due consideration of data available through other channels. Only so can philosophy fulfil its function of thinking consistently about the meaning of life *as a whole.*

The synoptic approach is empirical, but not in any narrowly limited sense. Starting from authority, which is second-hand truth mediated to us through first-hand experience, it regards the pronouncements of authority as something to be tested by further experience. Such experience may be intuitional or sensory; it usually is neither one alone but is bound up with life in all its complexity. If intuitional evidence is sought—or not being sought presses in upon us—it may come in the form of the moral imperative, or the artist's insights, or the mystic's vision. None of these evidences is to be thrust aside as irrelevant; each is to be subjected to further testing. One way of testing it—but not the only way—is the objective verifiability of sense experience and the drawing from it of scientific inference. Another—the pragmatic way—is to submit our fragmentary experience to the test of consequences in the more complete experience of life in the large and in the long. Not as a separate method to be used in isolation from the rest, but in conjunction with them all, is the test of logical consistency. The White Queen could believe six impossible things before breakfast, but not the philosopher with a conscience.

As an illustration of the synoptic approach I shall take a familiar problem probably settled for most of the readers of this book, but still debatable enough in many minds to be illustrative of clashing claims. This is the problem of man's biological ancestry.

For centuries before Darwin, at least since the days of

Anaxagoras, there have been people who believed in evolution. The authority accepted by the masses, however, was on the side of special creation until Darwin appeared. After 1859 the issue was clearly joined, for the authority of the Bible, as then interpreted, and the authority of the church was against man's animal ancestry and that of scientific thought was for it. One who tried to settle the problem on the basis of *authority only* found himself the prey of psychological rather than logical considerations, for he either continued from long association to hold the view accepted in his childhood or, if he changed it, he did so on the basis of hero-worship rather than cogency of argument.

In the midst of this clash of authorities, with a growing number of liberals in the church going over to the position affirmed by science, the method of one "say so" over against another was both corrupted and corrected by intuitional considerations. When the Darwinian theory was so interpreted as to exclude God, belittle man, and put man's most precious values into the discard, not only the religious but the ethical and æsthetic intuitions of spiritually-minded persons rose up against it. One finds in the poetry as in the theology of the past seventy-five years a fundamental intuitive unwillingness to let the highest human values be explained in subhuman terms. This resistance, on the one hand, retarded the advance of scientific truth, and on the other it purged nineteenth-century materialism of some of its cruder implications.

Meanwhile the frank acceptance of evolution by liberal religion in conjunction with spiritual values made for religious as well as intellectual progress. The death of William Jennings Bryan after the Dayton trial, victim of fidelity to a lost cause, is symbolic of the way intuition fights to the death; and whether its cross is a mark of shame or triumph depends on whether it has the truth-validating forces of the universe on its side. Often, as I believe to have been the case with Bryan, these "come mixed."

Neither authority nor intuition could settle the question, which was factually one of scientific evidence and spiritually one of interpretation of these facts. As the factual evidence piled up through knowledge of anatomy, embryology, paleontology, and many other fields, conflict waned. Pragmatically the theory of evolution worked as a unifying explanation of many otherwise disconnected phenomena, and the law of parsimony demanded its acceptance.

From the Darwinian *hypothesis,* as a guess or supposition to be tested, the evolutionary view passed into the stage of a *theory,* and now is generally accepted as *fact.* It is accepted by most people not on first-hand knowledge but on the testimony of those trusted to be credible authorities; and these in turn base their conclusions on the coherence of scientific evidence and the working value of this hypothesis as an explanation of empirical data. Intuition has nothing to do with the truth of the theory as scientific fact, but it has a great deal to do with the truth of the deductions for living which are drawn from it.

Any one of these approaches, taken alone, would yield either an incorrect or an inadequate conclusion. When brought into conjunction and allowed to correct each other, they make possible an important advance toward truth.

3. TRUTH AND VALUE

What I am advocating as the synoptic method is a form of the criterion of coherence. To many minds coherence connotes a barren logical consistency—a viewing of things with "the round glass eye of the Absolute." But what is needed to enable us to arrive at any truth—particularly truth in a field which relates to the whole of life—is a synoptic vision full of rich and many-sided content from which values are not excluded. When we have got all the evidence available—material and spiritual, short range and long range—we are able to draw a conclusion which is as near correct as we can get. We shall not then have absolute truth. But we shall have knowledge enough to enable us to advance toward more, with certainty enough to undergird our living as we go. This is all any man knows, and all he needs to know.

The last statement is perhaps reminiscent of Keats' cryptic words,

> Beauty is truth, truth beauty,—that is all
> Ye know on earth, and all ye need to know.

Whether Keats intended to identify truth and value I do not know. I do not intend so to identify them, though neither can be understood apart from the other. To cite again the illustration of the preceding section, the truth of biological evolution and the spiritual meaning of creation are not identical. Bryan in my judgment was right in one sphere but not the other. Nor are the existence of God and the spiritual meaning of God identical. It is possible to have a high measure of confidence in one of these without the other. But *the truth about a value is as important as any other truth;* and in morals and religion, impregnated in their every nature with values, to disregard values is to cut off an important part of the approach to truth. The synoptic method requires, therefore, that mystical, æsthetic and moral experience have their place along with scientific evidence.

4. THE LEGITIMACY OF SUPERNATURALISM

The term supernaturalism is full of pitfalls, not only for reasons earlier suggested, but because it may represent either an epistemological or a metaphysical position. It is with the former we are now mainly concerned, though the greater part of the remainder of the book will deal with the latter.

In a metaphysical sense, the term refers to the existence of a more-than-human and more-than-natural Controller of the universe and Determiner of destiny. In an epistemological sense, it implies approach to knowledge of this Being through other than the methods appropriate to a study of physical nature. For this "other than" there are many terms, but the best is the oldest and richest—namely, faith.

If faith were our *sole* approach to deity, the method followed could be neither empirical nor synoptic. Yet without some faith by which to appropriate revelation we could have knowledge neither of God *nor of anything else*.

Revelation, which is the correlate of faith on the objective side, permeates all knowing. Without revelation nothing would be given for our minds to act upon. I do not mean here revelation in a special religious sense, but "in the natural light of reason"—as natural a light as one may wish. The essential "givenness" of things is the starting-point of all knowledge, and knowledge of what is given is an appropriation of revelation. In the simplest act of sense experience, such as looking at a tree and seeing something there which from the standpoint of practical certainty one knows to exist, there is a response in our minds to what is objectively revealed.

The degree to which this appropriation of revelation falls short of absolute certainty, and therefore is in part inevitably a matter of faith, has been discussed in the preceding chapter. It would be easy to over-shoot the mark and affirm, as is often done, that the inevitability of faith in sense experience erases the problem with reference to religious experience. I believe that supernaturalism is valid in both fields, but that this does not justify hopping blithely from the conditions of one field to the other.

The philosopher of religion who has grappled most earnestly with this problem in our times is Professor Wieman. Supernaturalism, whether in its epistemological or metaphysical meaning, is not in my judgment antithetical to empiricism; but Professor Wieman thinks it is and rests his philosophy of religion upon this distinction. I accept his statement of the requirements of the empirical method, "that every belief be formed and tested by sensory observation, experimental behavior and rational inference."[2] I believe, however, that no sensory observation, and no experimental behavior, can be interpreted without the assumption of postulates which go beyond the bare occurrence of events in nature, and that rational inference requires at a minimum the faith that rational inference is trustworthy.

The extent to which it is possible to reach a supernaturalist conclusion by an empirical approach depends on the radicalness with which sensory observation, experimental behavior and rational inference are employed. Used part way, it leaves one with only such knowledge as can be gained through science. Employed all the way, or at least as far as we can take it, it makes a place for the data gleaned through all the avenues of a synoptic approach. If in this *thoroughgoing* use of empiricism we find data which can be satisfactorily accounted for only on the assumption of a more-than-human and more-than-natural deity, we need not hesitate to affirm that such a deity exists.[3]

A synoptic approach, starting from empirical foundations and employing both faith and rational inference to appropriate the "givenness" of revelation, points toward a

[2]"God Is More Than We Can Think" in *Christendom*, Spring, 1936.

[3]I believe that Professor Wieman is more of a supernaturalist than he will call himself. The word of Professor Roy Wood Sellars, quoted in *American Philosophies of Religion*, p. 264, seems to me at this point to speak the exact truth. "Upon this I think all naturalists are agreed [he writes in *The New Humanist*] that between naturalism and theism it is a case of either-or." For Professors Wieman and Meland to include such theists as Robert L. Calhoun and William K. Wright, along with themselves, among the naturalists seems to me to denature naturalism.

supernaturalist metaphysics. There is a difference in our knowledge of a tree and our knowledge of human nature, another difference in our knowledge of human nature and of God. Yet the difference lies not in method of procedure, but in the kind of data which objective reality gives to us when we employ radically the synoptic method.

5. A RECAPITULATION

The discussion thus far has centered about ideals, and while I have tried to show that the current assumption which sets up an antithesis between ideals and reality is false I have avoided making metaphysical claims for the objective validity, or cosmic status, of ideals. The remainder of the book will deal mainly with God and the relations of God to the ideals by which men live. Before going forward to examine the metaphysical questions involved in the problem of God, it may be well to look back over the ground which has been covered.

An examination of the current scene reveals a trend towards the dissolution of ideals. For this there are many causes, and various projected cures. Only a multiple approach toward creative idealism is adequate. More significant than the contemporary situation is the fact that, as human beings, we are all doomed by our nature to be a prey to evil, egocentric impulses and to profoundly disturbing emotions. Yet at the same time we are blessed by our human nature with the capacity to generate ideals by which to escape, in part, from our sin and limitation. These ideals are concepts of what ought to be, accepted by us as mandatory upon conduct. They are principles of action which have an emotional foundation and a volitional effect. They are in part attainable, though possibilities of further attainment are inexhaustible. They are not illusions. Though the question of whether they reflect the existence or the will of God may be held in abeyance, they have at least an important psychological reality which is attested by their potency. They have moral validity, though in varying degrees, and exercise a moral imperative. They come to us; yet we make them. Being not merely animal organisms but human personalities, we choose in part what ideals we shall follow and how far we shall follow them. We can live on the level of prudential adjustment, or socially respected character, or triumphant religion, but only on the third level do we truly attain salvation.

In spite of the fact that the majority of people feel no compelling desire to live on the level of triumphant religion, an empirical consideration of the condition of man and society suggests that this level must become a normative ideal. It can be achieved only by a dual emphasis upon life and thought, for an ideal is an idea made dynamic through feeling. The road to the emotional inception and galvanizing of ideals is through incarnation in life—a process achieved through prayer, through the redemptive power of suffering, through many other channels among which personal example and personal participation in vital action are indispensable. The road to religious knowledge, which is difficult because of the paradoxical fact that the most important knowledge is the least certain, can best be found through a synoptic approach which starts from empirical foundations and leads into a supernaturalist metaphysics.

Such synoptic supernaturalism does not give complete knowledge of religious truth, but it gives practical certainty through a joint consideration of scientific fact and man's value experiences. This knowledge, though incomplete, is all that is available by any method, and all that is needed for living triumphantly.

Truth and value are not to be identified, but neither are they to be viewed in isolation. A synoptic approach necessitates consideration of all the ways of knowing—authority, intuition, scientific observation, practical consequences and logical consistency. This approach, though rooted in faith which is the correlate of revelation, uses rational inference radically and inclusively rather than partially. So used, it finds a supernaturalist epistemology legitimate and points toward a supernaturalist metaphysics. If upon following its lead we find validity in the idea of God, we shall have discovered firm ground to stand upon while moving toward the creative idealism of triumphant religion.

Chapter IX

THE EXISTENCE OF GOD

THE CHAPTERS thus far have indicated some channels by which idealism can become creative and a dependable body of religious knowledge can be established. Little has been said about God for two reason: pragmatically and pedagogically, it is preferable to begin in areas less controversial; philosophically, the approach must be empirical if it is to be established on intellectually solid foundations. However, by a frank acceptance of the term supernaturalism which has metaphysical as well as epistemological connotations, I have suggested that the discussion would lead into a position affirming a theistic position.

I shall not until a later chapter attempt to define what I mean by God, save in the general sense of a Transcendent Being regarded as divine, worshiped, and thought to exercise significant control over the universe. By Transcendent Being I do not intend to deny the divine immanence, but only to suggest that God cannot be identified with nature. To equate God wholly with physical or human nature is, in my judgment, to eliminate him; for these we have anyway, and if we have these only, God is naught. There are drawbacks in deferring further definition, but it is necessary for the reason that we cannot in any precise manner say what God is until we survey the evidence by which to judge that he is at all.

The term supernaturalism, as was earlier intimated, has long had a good deal of crude superstition connected with it. At least a part of the reason why both the word and the theology it represents have become unpopular is an emotional aversion to the accretions which have gathered about it. The way to overcome this aversion is to banish superstition from its connotation by as inclusive an inquiry as possible.

It was suggested in the preceding chapter that a synoptic approach to truth involves a canvass of the evidence attainable through authority, intuition, natural science, a survey of practical consequences and the test of logical consistency. In this chapter and the next we shall examine authority, two types of intuition—mystical and moral, and the cosmological evidences of God's existence. I shall not make a separate treatment of pragmatic and logical considerations, but shall hope to consider them throughout the argument.

I. THE EVIDENCE OF AUTHORITY

An important, and in fact indispensable, approach to truth is the way of authority. This has fallen under condemnation in a scientific age, but nobody lives or learns without it. If the amount of information accumulated by the normal five-year-old had all to be discovered *ab initio* by his own experience, he could live out his three score years and ten, or hypothetically attain to the ripe old age of Methuselah, and still know a good deal less than he has acquired by the kindly aid of parental authority by his fifth birthday. Perhaps Romulus and Remus, suckled by their wolf-mother, grew up in an authority-less world, but no human being does so outside of fable.

If authority, then, is so indispensable to the accumulation of the knowledge by which we live as educated and at least semi-civilized persons, why do we so shrink from it in the field of religion? Mainly because authority to be dependable has to be trusted with discrimination, and there has been inadequate discrimination for many centuries in this field. The fact that judgments in the field of politics are equally undiscriminating, but more popularly acceptable, is a *tu quoque* argument which does not exonerate religion from error.

The rejection of authority in religion has been more widespread in the past generation than at any previous period in history, though at present there are signs of a resurgence of a new "age of faith." Some of the causes of this rejection were surveyed in Chapter II. The slight extent to which economic disturbance has been responsible is evidenced by the fact that Walter Lippmann's *Preface to Morals,* which still remains the most trenchant description in print of the processes by which the rejection came about, was published in the spring of 1929. In this he writes:

The evidences of these greater difficulties lie all about us: in the brave and brilliant atheists who have defied the Methodist God, and have become very nervous; in the women who have emancipated themselves from the tyranny of fathers, husbands and homes, and with the intermittent but expensive help of a psychoanalyst, are now enduring liberty as interior decorators; in the young men and women who are world-weary at twenty-two; in the multitudes who drug themselves with pleasure; . . . in the millions, at last free to think without fear of priest or policeman, who have made the moving-pictures and the popular newspapers what they are.

These are the prisoners who have been released. They ought to be very happy. They ought to be serene and composed. They are free to make their own lives. There are no conventions, no tabus, no gods, priests, princes, fathers, or revelations which they must accept. Yet the result is not so good as they thought it would be. The prison door is wide open. They stagger out into trackless space under a blinding sun. They find it nerve-racking.[1]

The young people here described are accepting all the while, of course, the authority of those companions, teachers, popular writers, *et al* who say there is nothing in religion or in ideals. The more brilliant the diction or the more attractive the personality, the more readily the authority is accepted. Walter Lippmann himself exercises more jurisdiction over many of them than do the priests and policemen here referred to.

This fact is important because it suggests that there is one type of authority from which, try as we will, we never fully break away. This is the authority of individual personality. Let us see what relevance this has to the idea of God.

a. The authority of personality

I place the authority of personality before the authority of Bible or creed, both because it is inherently more au-

[1]*Op. cit.,* p. 6.   By permission of The Macmillan Co.

thentic, and because it is pragmatically more certain of acceptance. This is not in any sense to discredit Biblical or creedal truth, but to suggest that these get their meaning from what they reflect about persons and what they do in the lives of persons.

I have said before that incarnation in life is indispensable to the generation of ideals of triumphant religion. What I am saying now is that the evidence of incarnation in life is also a road to the truth about God. I mean not merely a road to *acceptance* of the idea of God, although it is this; but a road toward its validation. This could be illustrated endlessly from the lives of persons who have lived greatly; I shall cite only one instance. When S. Parkes Cadman was dying in a Roman Catholic hospital in Plattsburgh, the sisters said of him, "We have never seen any one like him." What Doctor Cadman believed about the Bible or the creeds sank into the background, and all differences were obscured in this spontaneous witness to the greatness of a person who grounded his life, as he preached his last sermon, upon the words, "Being justified by faith, we have peace with God through our Lord Jesus Christ." When people live like this, there is still a theoretical margin of possibility that they stake their lives on an illusion, but the universe is all a madhouse if they do.

The Bible is the world's greatest record of a growing spiritual experience; the creeds embody the intellectual formulation of living faith. Out of these two come most of what we know about religion, and rightly interpreted they are reservoirs of truth as well as power. But we cannot use them in the old way. When rejected, they are no longer authorities. The suspicion has arisen, growing in many minds to a certainty, that what our fathers held to be the word of God is the speech of many variant voices. Some of these speak with the ring of truth, others in tones vapid or raucous, and there is lack of clear discernment as to what to take and what to reject. In this uncertainty there is too much of wholesale rejection. Such rejection is best corrected by a demonstration, both intellectual and vital, of what the Bible and the creeds mean in terms of human living.

b. The authority of history

A second valid use of authority is the appeal to history. History, like creeds and catechisms, is under suspicion in an age geared mainly to the present. Yet there, spread out before us if we will read it, lies the record of five millenniums of civilization, two of these under the ægis of Christianity. It is quite the custom to refer to this record of history for evidence that all religions are much alike—full of superstition, a sop to man's sentimental yearning for security, and a reinforcement of whatever social standards may be current. I suggest that we look at history more objectively, and if we can divest ourselves sufficiently of prejudice, we shall read there the record of a growing pattern of ideals of humanitarianism and good will, nourished more often by religion than any other agency and nourished more effectively by the Christian religion than by any other faith. This, in fairness, needs to be said whenever we point out the reciprocal truth that

Christianity after nineteen centuries has not yet banished war, economic oppression or racial discrimination from the attitudes and actions of the great numbers of its adherents.

By the entrance to the library of the University of Rochester are carved two inscriptions. On one side this:

Here is the history of human ignorance, error, superstition, folly, war and waste, recorded by human intelligence for the admonishment of wise ages still to come.

And on the other, this:

Here is the history of Man's hunger for Truth, Goodness and Beauty—leading him slowly on through flesh to spirit, from bondage to freedom, from war to peace.

In these two summaries is stated the paradox of history, the revelation that in the race, as in individual man, is a union of original sin and original goodness, of finitude and infinity. In man's upward climb his hunger for eternal values has been "leading him slowly through flesh to spirit, from bondage to freedom, from war to peace." One may read this record, as he may scan the heavens, without reference to deity. It is no more necessary to talk about God in a course in history, considered as a social science, than in a course in astronomy. To do so would confuse the scientific enterprise. But if history is considered in its total setting, the record of human aspiration and achievement becomes the record of a cosmic process wherein God is the source and goal of values.

c. The authority of Jesus

These two, the authority of personal triumphant living and the record of increasing triumph of spiritual ideals in the on-going processes of history, meet in a third ground of authority. This is the authority of Jesus. There have been theological discussions a-plenty, which need not here be reviewed, about the relations of the historical Jesus to the Christ of faith. The point which emerges clear from any discussion save the most biased is that the earthly life of Jesus of Nazareth is the most important occurrence in the entire history of the human race. It is no accident that from the reputed year of his birth we date our calendar. Furthermore, the recognition of Jesus as God by millions of people since that time, whether their recognition was intuitive and spontaneous or calculated and critical, has been the basis of a living perpetuation of his influence as the Christ of faith.

As to how far the life and death of Jesus Christ may be taken as manifestation of a special divinity with a special mission, opinions differ. It is certain that to these the Christian Church owes its origins and its power; it is not certain which of its numerous doctrines of the incarnation and atonement is most authentic. I believe that a sinless and sacrificial life of such utter purity as Jesus attained to is inexplicable except as the manifestation of a divinity which is not only supreme, but in a certain sense unique.

III

But if we put as far to one side as possible controversial issues and limit attention to what is generally agreed upon by Christians, respectful atheists and scoffers, we have a minimum from which a deduction of maximum importance can be drawn. For any person to *live as Jesus lived* and *speak as he spoke* would be impossible unless a more-than-human and more-than-natural agency operated through him. In the personality of Jesus and its perpetual impact on human life we find a union of the individual with the historical which has transcendent significance.

In Jesus Christ is the supreme manifestation of God. Philosophers of religion have shrunk from saying so, lest they be charged with being theologians. But any cosmological approach which leaves out this fact lacks completeness. Furthermore, it lacks certainty and dynamic, for it is not an argument *about* God, but a living manifestation of God, which transforms life.

If current life is to be rescued from a morass of meaninglessness, it will be in terms of many things, but foremost among them in terms of a new appreciation of Jesus. We started our discussion by pointing out that the world is very largely in a state of bedlam. Perhaps it is not aside the point to remind ourselves that the original meaning of bedlam was Bethlehem. It was from the hospital of St. Mary of Bethlehem[2] that the word came into being. If sanity comes out of bedlam in our day, it will be mainly through that perennial revelation of divinity which ap-

2The priory of St. Mary of Bethlehem in London, founded in 1247, came to be used in the early fifteenth century as a hospital for the insane.

peared in human form at Bethlehem at the turning-point of history.

2. THE EVIDENCE OF MYSTICISM

We pass now to a brief consideration of mysticism as an approach to the validation of the idea of God. To turn to mysticism is not to leave authority, for the mystic's vision is to him indubitably authoritative.

Mysticism is not popular in our day, either in theological or in "vulgar" circles. Its greatest American exponent writes of it, whimsically, that it "has been out late nights and has come back 'bedraggled.' "[3] And undoubtedly, some forms are psychologically unhealthy as well as epistemologically and theologically of dubious value.

First, it is necessary to clear the word of popular misconceptions. To many minds mysticism connotes mystery—a connotation which has some justification from its historical connection with the mystery religions. But most of those who so stigmatize it do not know this fact, and they use the term, as they use "metaphysics," to mean something vague and messy. While there is mystery about mysticism, as about everything in existence, it has no monopoly on it and mystery is by no means its distinguishing trait.

Another misconception of the word is to confuse it with occultism of the spiritistic type. Whatever there may, or may not, be in such psychic phenomena as automatic writing and spirit rappings, these are not mysticism in any reputable sense.

[3]Rufus Jones: *The Testimony of the Soul*, p. 200.

Two other meanings the term has, both connoting types of experience described and defended by the great mystics. As I shall try to show presently, they are not of equal value, either epistemologically or psychologically; but both are types of experience correctly called mysticism. Failure to distinguish between them has besmeared many an argument.

The first of these is the *via negativa,* which is the way of mystical ecstasy. This was the great early meaning of the term, as set forth by Pseudo-Dionysius, Plotinus, and to a considerable extent by Augustine. It is based on the assumption that God is *totaliter aliter*—so far above man in his transcendence that no road leads to him through the human mind. Only by a "flight of the alone to the Alone," as Plotinus put it, or by a leap out of one's own personality into the "divine dark" could the gulf be spanned. Descriptions of the hypnotic, semi-conscious state in which such ecstatic union was experienced are familiar in the literature of mysticism. Augustine does not claim to have had a full-fledged ecstasy. He suggestively describes its elements, however, when he says of himself and his mother Monica, "We came to our minds, and we passed beyond them with the utmost leap of our hearts." "In one trembling flash, without intermediary, we touched the Eternal Wisdom."[4]

Such ecstatic, albeit abnormal, states are not devoid of religious value. Nor do they belong wholly to a by-gone day. While I should not like to link too closely the depth of experience of the great mystics and the phe-

[4]Quoted by Rufus Jones, *op. cit.,* p. 193.

nomena of present-day untutored religious experience, I have witnessed demonstrations of mystical ecstasy in the revivalism of a Holiness camp-meeting. In the semi-hypnotic behavior of many of the participants there were expressions, both verbal and kinæsthetic, which left no doubt of the total abandon and utter happiness of the worshipers. There was apparently an almost complete self-forgetfulness as attention was directed toward the object of worship, and indubitable assurance of the presence and saving power of the Divine Being to whom adoration was being addressed.

It may be argued by the more sophisticated that such expressions reveal simply the cultural crudity of those who engage in them. However, whatever may be said of gullibility or grotesqueness, the dominant characteristic of such expressions is intensity of religious feeling—a fact related to cultural considerations only in that the inhibitions which coerce most of us into more sober conduct are there inoperative. I have no wish to commend such experiences as something to be generally cultivated. Yet it is easy to overlook the fact that there is in them moral value as well as emotional stimulation. The only individual I know personally who claims never to have been unhappy, and whose daily life certainly manifests an almost totally undisturbed serenity, is a half-crippled middle-aged woman to whom attendance at camp-meeting is "meat and drink," life's supremely joyous experience.

But while such experiences of ecstatic mysticism have for the worshiper an agreeable feeling-tone, and for his conduct usually a mixture of good and bad consequences, little can be said for them as validations of the reality of God. Intensity of subjective feeling may elicit respect or derision, but it convinces no one who does not share that feeling.

The second type of mysticism may be termed affirmative mysticism in contrast with the negative type of the ecstatic leap toward the divine. The emotional accompaniments and outward expressions are milder in form. The worshiper enters no hypnotic state, but in his communion with Another he feels himself, paradoxically, to be in the immediate presence of a Transcendent Being. Far from losing his self-consciousness, he finds it heightened and enhanced. He feels within him an insurge of power which must find expression in action. The practical results of such mysticism are twofold: first, to enable the worshiper to overcome the cloven and chaotic character of his world and find peace for his soul; second, to furnish both motivation and dynamic energy by which to live more effectively in the light of his ideals. These results are intimated in classic words of which the meaning is often obscured but never exhausted:

In the world ye have tribulation: but be of good cheer; I have overcome the world.
I can do all things through Christ which strengtheneth me.

It is evident that this kind of mysticism is of very great value for living. It is, in substance, what we were talking about when we said that prayer is an indispensable approach to the incarnation in life of triumphant religion. It is this kind of mysticism which gives validity to the "principle of alternation,"[5] to the rhythm of worship and action. Without it, religious experience would die for lack of being watered at its roots.

The value of the experience proves that it is worth cultivating—if this can be done without inner hypocrisy. But what does it show about the truth of the mystic's certainty of God's presence?

It does not indubitably prove God to be real. One may still ask whether it is God, or the *idea* of God that the worshiper communes with. The mystic's certainty has to be reinforced by all other tests, particularly the pragmatic, before it can be affirmed as true.

Though it be asserted that what the worshiper communes with is the idea of God rather than God himself, this is not necessarily to brand the experience as illusion. In an analogous sense to that in which we never directly experience another human being's personality, but only its impact upon our own, we can say that in mystical communion we *infer* God rather than experience him. But in our experience of another human being, there is within our experience of self an indubitable awareness of a "not-self" that we call another person. Usually we do not stop to ask how we know. Intuitive certainty seems enough. But if you become critical and begin to inquire *how you know* that it is really another person, and not a figment of your own imagination in

[5] W. E. Hocking: *The Meaning of God in Human Experience*, Chap. XXVIII.

delirium or dream, that is talking with you, the problem becomes more difficult.[6]

If, however, you pursue the question, you will probably decide that your intuitive certainty of the presence of another human being can be put to certain valid tests. There is a real person present when things happen which would not otherwise happen, and when everything about the idea fits together coherently without any gaps at the edges. The murderer you dream about does not kill you, nor does the benefactor of your air-castle leave you a fortune. The scenario-writer may put his character to sleep in the first act to dream the rest of the story, but when he wakes up there has to be a break in continuity which gives away the illusion.

From application of these tests of coherence and consequences to the mystic's vision, intuitive certainty receives reinforcement and purging. Most of the great mystics admit the necessity of such testing. St. Teresa of Avila remarks that if some person "were to tell me that a person with whom I had just conversed, and whom I knew well, was not that person, but that I was deluding myself, and that they knew it, I should certainly trust them rather than my own eyes. But if that person left with me certain jewels—and if, possessing none previ-

[6]The old rhyme, descriptive of much epistemological speculation, is relevant at this point.

> The centipede was happy, quite
> Until the frog, for fun,
> Asked, "Pray, which leg comes after which?"
> This worked his mind to such a pitch,
> He lay exhausted in the ditch
> Considering how to run.

ously, I held the jewels in my hand as pledges of a great love—and if I were now rich, instead of poor as before . . ."[7] she would have to believe. The jewels she refers to are tenderness, joy, humility, peace, insight. "The divine locutions," she says, "instruct us without loss of time, and we understand matters which seem to require a month on our part to arrange."[8]

This is a long way from saying that the mystic's vision is all the evidence of God we need. For the practical demands of living it may be, for a philosophy of religion it is not. Yet one may keep within the bounds of philosophic caution and affirm that religious experience gives data more important to religious truth than any which comes from sense experience. To fail to take it into account is to leave out the main subject under consideration—a procedure which no scientist in any other field would regard as very scientific!

The avenues to God thus far considered—the way of authority, whether personal, historical or Christological, and the way of mystical intuition—are what we ordinarily mean by "faith." We may, of course, mean by faith something much cruder, a credulous acceptance of whatever happens to be told. This kind of faith it is not worth while to consider except for purposes of rejection. But it is as important to recognize the empirical evidence which becomes available through the kind of faith we have been discussing as it is to reject the faith of credulous assumption.

Whether faith even in its most valid forms can ever lead

[7] *Autobiography*, XXVIII, 19.   [8] *Ibid.*, XXV, 12.

to truth is a question about which doctors disagree. I trust it is clear that I do not claim for religious faith the validity of proof. We cannot by it come to absolute certainty. But without it, even practical certainty is hidden from us.

With authority and religious experience as important starting-points, we must go to the sciences and to the moral imperative for further evidences of God. These will be examined in the next chapter.

Chapter X

TO GOD THROUGH SCIENCE AND
MORAL IDEALS

In the preceding chapter some considerations were presented which tend to validate the idea of God from the standpoint of authority and of religious experience. Declining to rest the case on Biblical or creedal authority alone which—however potent to a person on the inside of the Christian tradition—has little weight with one on the outside, I tried to show that there are other types of authority less open to cavil. One does not ordinarily speak of "empirical authority," but this seems to me a legitimate term by which to describe the type which has its dynamic center in individual personality, in the record of history, or in the union of personality with history in Jesus.

Some aspects of mysticism were surveyed. After clearing away some débris from the meaning of the term, we found it to apply either to the *via negativa* of ecstatic flight from the human into the divine, or to the milder but more potent experience ordinarily termed worship, communion, or simply "religious experience." The former type has something of moral value, the latter has more with less admixture of evil. Neither experience proves God to be real; but the subjective certainty which it imparts to the worshiper, though requiring to be further tested, nevertheless affords important data which cannot, without incompleteness, be omitted from consideration.

Before passing to examine what light may be thrown on the idea of God by man's moral intuitions, it will be fruitful to see how far we can get by way of the natural sciences.

I. THE EVIDENCE OF SCIENCE

The synoptic method requires that the validity of the idea of God be examined not only in the light of the best possible authority and the sanest, most triumphant mystical experience, but in the light of science. This does not mean that through science, whose field is preeminently the natural, we can expect to find direct evidence of the supernatural. To expect to find it would be misplaced confidence. But it is also misplaced confidence to suppose that science gives us direct evidence of a physical order. What science does is *to make rational inferences from observable data,* and on this basis to build up a great—and very valuable—structure of probabilities. We shall, therefore, be keeping within the bounds of scientific method in its larger meaning (though not in its more limited connotation) if we study the world to see what is there which might throw light on the idea of God, and then make rational inferences from what is found. The danger is, of course, that we shall "rationalize" instead of being rational. But since this is a danger which besets every other attempt to draw inferences, the philosopher of religion need not timidly retreat because of it.

One who trains his telescope upon the heavens or his microscope upon a mass of living tissue will not see God there. What he will see is suns and spiral nebulæ, cells and colloids, from which he infers (never directly observes) a natural order of things. The *order* seems certain, and grows increasingly certain as science advances. Its *naturalness* depends on the interpretation attached to the word. To say that anything is "natural" may mean that it is physical, or that it stands in a fixed system of causal relations, or that it is self-caused and self-contained. The first meaning does not necessarily presuppose the other two, nor do the first two presuppose the third.

To orderliness, as a characteristic of the physical universe, is added far more beauty than utility requires and, in general, nourishing support for the physical existence of living organisms. In this order there is regularity; there is also spontaneity and accident. It looks like a universe made both for dependable continuity of existence and for adventure—perhaps even for tragic adventure.

In the order, the beauty, the utility and the variability of the physical world is found an interrelated, complex whole of which it is difficult to believe an accidental collocation of atoms is the explanation. If deity is not its source, something else is which has some of the most important functions we ascribe to deity. I have listened to discussions of this theme which sounded as if one were trying to extrude God to introduce a godlike substitute.

Let us look briefly at the natural order within each of its three areas—the physical, the biological, and the social.

a. The physical sciences

In the fields of physics, chemistry, geology, astronomy and their sub-sciences, there is, if anywhere, evidence to substantiate a mechanistic view. There is an important sense in which Bertrand Russell is right when he says that "omnipotent matter rolls on its relentless way." I see no evidence that either faith or prayer will turn aside the path of a hurricane, and factually, I suppose Clarence Darrow was right when he tried to make Bryan admit at the Dayton trial that if the sun had stood still over the vale of Ajalon for half a day the earth would have collapsed and been converted into a molten mass of matter. But the sun does not stand still, and the earth to date remains in its basic structure intact. That there should be orderly phenomena by which we can be assured that

> while the earth remaineth, seed-time and harvest, and cold and heat, and summer and winter, and day and night, shall not cease,

seems to me more important than the correlative fact that *within these orderly phenomena* there are juxtapositions of circumstance by which come droughts and consequent famines, freezing cold and suffocating heat. This is not to suggest that formal orderliness is more important than human values, but that orderliness even though not conducive to values in every detail is more beneficial *on the whole* to human values than a chaotic world could possibly be. In the field of the physical sciences there are evidences of a rationality which substantiates belief not only in an ordering but a value-loving deity.

Much is being made in theological circles of the principle of indeterminacy as an answer to the mechanistic argument. It is possible to overdo its importance to theology. It makes scientifically respectable what philosophers have long believed, that there is contingency and novelty in the universe. Yet however true it may be that within the atom there are interruptions in continuity, *the world in which men live* is still a world of cause and effect. It is more important to find God manifest in the causally related phenomena of such a world than either in miracle or in quantum physics.

b. The life sciences

Regarding the life sciences the most important thing to be said has now become a commonplace in liberal theology: namely, that biological evolution is an argument *for* God and not against him. This point needs to be elaborated and given spiritual meaning until it seeps its way down to the masses who do not yet believe it and who through unbelief are left in spiritual confusion as science increasingly takes it for granted. The point, however, requires demonstration rather than argument; for it is obvious that, once one has divested himself of the shackles of literalistic Biblical interpretation, he can believe in a God of long purposes as readily as in one that creates in six days through fiat.

As in the field of inanimate physical nature, the way living organisms have developed presents an argument for

God but also raises a question not to be easily answered. As there is a problem in the existence of destructive hurricanes and droughts within an orderly cosmos, so is there a problem in the excessive waste and pain in animal life. Nature, apparently careful of the type but careless of the individual, advances through slow steps, and the trail is strewn with blood. I recall a student's remarking in semi-sardonic vein, "Yes, I think there must be a God—at least, something that makes the big bugs eat the little ones."

A God who did this only would be no God. What, then, shall we say? For more extensive discussion of the problem of evil we must wait for another chapter. But it may be said here in anticipation that in the process of teleological, creative advance, there seems to be evidence that God's will is being both partially wrought out and partially thwarted.

There is evidence of creative evolution, of the emergence of new forms not necessitated by their antecedents. In these emergents there are not only more complex forms of life but those which, being more capable of appreciating values, are themselves more *valuable*. A dog is worth more than a mosquito because it knows more; it experiences more affection; it responds more intelligently and attractively to its world. Yet a human infant is worth vastly more than a dog. The order of ascending levels which we find revealed in the biological ongoing is as it ought to be in a world directed by a deity working toward—and possibly beyond—the level of human personality as the goal of evolution.

In the upward swing from insensate to sentient, from

sentient to conscious, from conscious to valuing forms of life, there is evidence of a more-than-natural within the natural. Again the evidence falls short of proof, but it looks as if a God of values were directing the process.

c. The social sciences

In the field of the social sciences, we find evidence which presents a more conclusive and at the same time a more disputable argument for the existence of God. The social scientists seem in general to find less place for God than do those whose fields are in the physical sciences. At least part of the reason may be that social phenomena have so long been naïvely regarded as direct evidence of God that in reaction, having discovered the psychological, biological, and physical causes of many of these phenomena, the social scientists tend to fall prey to the genetic fallacy and assume that God is non-existent.

Looking at society with a long look backward, there is much empirical evidence to substantiate belief in a value-loving Controller of destiny. Social, like biological, evolution coheres with the concept of a God of long purposes, leading us slowly "through flesh to spirit, from bondage to freedom, from war to peace." There is nothing in the record of social evolution to substantiate the optimistic nineteenth century doctrine of automatic or unbroken progress. We sing sometimes over-blithely:

> Forward through the ages,
> In unbroken line,
> Move the faithful spirits
> At the call divine.

127

In reality the line is broken at many points, and progress comes by streaks and patches. There neither is, nor can we hope to have, "the progress of mankind onward and upward forever" if we mean by this that there are no set-backs in the process. Evolution might be defined as an age-long process of going forward a foot at a time and slipping back only eleven inches.

Yet the significant thing is that in spite of broken lines, and potholes worn deep by whirlpools in the stream of progress, *progress comes.* History surveyed in retrospect is as we should expect to find it in a world directed by a God of values who works toward goals but is impeded as he goes by human ignorance and sin.

Looking around us also to get a cross-section of time, we find a mixture of divine and demonic forces operative in human nature which in their out-working give evidence of God. The negative evidence of God's power, long submerged under a too optimistic view of the world, is reasserting itself in a day of chaos, and preachers are again proclaiming that "whatsoever a man soweth, that shall he also reap." One of the most clear-cut notes in modern (not modernist) theology is that "God is not mocked," that God is a God of wrath and justice as unmistakably as he is a God of love and tender mercy. We see fresh evidence that no society or culture can endure which persistently thwarts the moral ways of the universe, for the forces of aggrandizement by which it climbs to power are the very forces which eventually destroy it. It is written in "the signs of the times," more clearly than in any signs of the heavens by which our forefathers thought to read destiny in the stars, that there are eternal moral laws in the structure of things.

It is dearly-bought knowledge that men cannot wage a World War, or build a society on greed, or worship the nation as God without paying the price—but if we learn the lesson it may be worth the cost. Had the words spoken by the Hebrew prophets been heard and heeded, it might not be necessary now to learn by experience what they so clearly saw and said.

2. THE EVIDENCE OF THE MORAL IMPERATIVE

This is the appropriate point at which to task how much of evidence for God we find in man's capacity to live by moral ideals. We earlier made much mention of the psychological reality of ideals, but refused from this either to assert or deny their metaphysical objectivity. The question, which would have been out of order before, is now relevant.

We said that in man there is an endless conflict going on. This conflict is a struggle between good and evil impulses which are partly native to us, partly acquired, sometimes dormant, and never fully eradicated. It is a conflict also in which our natural desire for a smooth-going life is frustrated by tendencies to fear, loneliness and bewilderment. Both sin and limitation corrupt our living. What enables good to triumph and release in some measure to take place is not primarily a set of physical forces but the capacity to live by a body of value-judgments.

In so far as man lives triumphantly, he lives by inner supports which are intangible and super-physical yet judged by their potency are indubitably real.

To say that man has ideals, or that ideals determine the higher reaches of his life, is of course quite different from saying that these speak to him of God. They may be analyzed psychologically into an exercise of memory, imagination, reason and will without saying anything at all about God. But when one asks the metaphysical question as to *why there should be creatures in the world* who have the power to surmount physical limitation and biological impulse to live by intangible ideals, the possibilities reduce to three. Human beings are the product of matter thrown together by chance—"a fortuitous concourse of atoms," or they are the product of the systematic action of an impersonal force, or they are the product of the creative agency of a mind which has concern for order and values. That chance should have given rise to man, even in his biological nature, is an hypothesis not easy to defend if one takes seriously the limited probability of a given outcome in any act of chance as simple as that of a throw of dice or a deal at cards. That the vastly more complex human organism—to say nothing of human intelligence—is the result of accidental "permutations and combinations" is a thesis less reasonable than the second alternative, that man is the product of an impersonal force which works systematically. But how the personal could emerge from the impersonal, the mental from the non-mental, the moral from the non-moral, is something which no exponent of this view has adequately made clear. The third alternative, that man is able to set goals and work toward them because his creator is of like nature, is a position which does not rest on analogy only but is supported by observation of the cosmic process. If there is a God of long purposes and moral values, one of the ways in which he works is presumably the creation of creatures able to project ideals into the future and labor to bring them to pass.

The argument from human personality converges with the moral argument for God, for man is most distinctively a creature of moral ideals. This approach through the moral imperative, however, is more valid on foundations laid by Paul than on those of Kant. "I ought, therefore I can" does not stand up under scrutiny. There are many things our deeper moral intuitions tell us we ought to do which we either cannot do at all or can do but feebly. Some of these meet barriers within ourselves, some in the evils of an iniquitous and vastly complex social order. It is a true teaching of the Gospel that having done all that we can, we are still unprofitable servants.

It is when man feels his helplessness, yet in the midst of futility knows that he is not defeated because God is on his side, that the argument from the moral imperative becomes most meaningful. With this insight a man is able to look at himself and say, "The evil which I would not, that I do"; he is able to look at the world and say "The whole creation groaneth and travaileth in pain together until now"; he is able to look at God and say, "We are more than conquerors through him that loved us."

So vital is this fact of the moral imperative to religion

that we could rest the case for God's existence on this fact alone, if we needed to, and still have solid standing-ground. This does not mean that every prompting of conscience is indubitably God's will. One may find God through conscience with clear vision, or "through a glass darkly." The issue at stake at this point is not, "Is every impulse of conscience the voice of God?" Rather it is, "Is the *fact* of conscience significant?" It is a conviction of the Christian faith, reinforced by the power of ideals in experience, that to the latter question we are entitled to reply in the affirmative. The insight that "what is highest in spirit is also deepest in nature"[1] is a signpost pointing towards divinity.

Professor Hocking has put this idea in words which deserve to become classic. I shall quote them.

The essence of the matter is this—and I rest the case on it. There is such a thing as conscience: what is it? Not a racial memory, but a sense of obligation that lights on this or that course when reflection has detached us for a moment from the clamor of self-interest. Is conscience a luxury, a psychological accident, an economic lubricant, an ephemeral sentiment induced by an indifferent world? Or is it a companionship, an intimation of destiny, a perception that human choices have some bearing upon an eternal order of being? To suppose that in some way conscience represents the nature of things makes all the difference in a man's life; to have such men as its components makes all the difference in the life of a civilization.[2]

[1] W. P. Montague, *Belief Unbound*, p. 6.
[2] "Does Civilization *Still* Need Religion?" in *Christendom*, Autumn, 1935.

The argument from man's moral imperative reinforces the argument from evidences of teleogical creative advance in the larger stream of society to which we have earlier made reference. Viewed either from the standpoint of the presence of constructive moral ideals or their absence, the argument comes out at the same place. Where ideals of love and justice prevail to a significant degree, there is inner stability and progress in the arts; where acquisitiveness and the will to power are regnant, chaos follows. Prosperity is no evidence of God's favor, as the old Semitic concept would have it; but peace—when peace is built upon fellowship and not upon fear—may well be an evidence of God's presence. Conversely, the large-scale presence of chaos, whether expressed in war or the general loss of a sense of the meaning of life, gives evidence that a God of values not only guides but judges the human moral enterprise.

3. AN INCLUSIVE VIEW

We are ready now to try to put together the evidence accessible through various channels. The evidence through one channel would be of real, though limited, value; the converging evidence from many channels points toward a transcendent, yet immanent, ordering, value-loving deity.

Following the inevitable road of authority, we found evidence of God's existence in personal triumphant living, in the witness of history, and in the union of these in the authority of Jesus Christ. The way of the mystics' vision divides into two paths—the negative way of an ecstatic leap in the dark toward union with the Great

Unknown, the affirmative way of positive vital communion. Put to the test of consistency and pragmatic consequences, the second of these is an essential step towards establishing the validity of belief in God.

The evidence from the sciences was considered on three levels: the inanimate, the biological, and the human. Physical nature reveals an orderliness and a beauty which is most readily explained as the work of an ordering, value-loving deity, though the occurrence of physical phenomena disastrous to human values suggests the presence of limitation upon God's control. Similarly in the life sciences there is evidence of creative advance which substantiates the existence of such a deity, though excess of pain and waste again suggests limitations of his power. In the field of human social relations, the evidences of gradual, though uneven, moral progress point to a God of goals, as the consequences of thwarting the ways of the universe point to a God of judgment. The presence in man of a moral imperative which overcomes powerful natural impulses and enables him to live with self-direction, and in some measure with triumph, gives evidence of a God of moral values and moral power who labors for man's redemption, but who will not invade the freedom by which man makes or mars his destiny.

Further considerations as to the nature of this deity and his dealings with men must be examined in the chapters which follow.

Chapter XI

WHAT GOD IS NOT

THE TWO preceding chapters have shown that an empirical starting-point leads by the synoptic approach toward the conclusion that a transcendent, ordering, value-loving deity is in significant control of the universe. In these chapters I carefully avoided using the adjective *personal* to describe this deity, for the reason that *personal,* like *supernatural,* is an ambiguous term—a "weasel word" which has to be given content before it can be safely used. I believe God to be personal, as I believe him to be supernatural, in a certain sense, but not in the sense attached to the term by many people.

In order to lead up to a statement of what God is, I shall begin by saying what God is not.

I. IS GOD A PERSON?

In the first place, *God is not the crudely anthropomorphic deity which naïve thought often imagines him to be.* This is so obvious as not to require statement, save for the fact that great numbers of people still picture God with a human body, or relinquishing this picture as they emerge from childhood, have nothing left. At least, they still go on blithely teaching their children that God is up in heaven (which means the sky), looking down upon us, keeping watch of every act, perhaps also recording these acts in a great book for use at the Day of Judgment. The danger to adult religion which comes from such picture-thinking is great unless care is taken to see that a proper transition is made to a more spiritual concept.

A citation from a student's paper which suggests this confusion will perhaps bear repeating:

When I was very young I was afraid of the dark—which meant that I was afraid of ghosts. But of all the ghosts I had ever heard of, the one I was most afraid of was the Holy Ghost. He was in my Sunday-school lesson and in the prayers the minister said, and so I assumed that one so well known must be the worst ghost of them all. . . .

I can't clearly remember what the rest of my early religious thoughts were. It was fear that stamped the Holy Ghost on my memory. The angels in the stained glass windows in the church fascinated me. I rather imagined I could see clearly an endless room with a soft billowy cloud for a floor and a bright blue sky for a ceiling, a bewhiskered gentleman seated on a throne in the center with pink and blue and lavender angels (as in the window) floating around.

Sometimes I wonder if our childhood fancies aren't the happiest to keep anyway, for I soon grew out of this vision in pastels and had nothing left but a jumbled, muddled idea of nothing at all.[1]

It is probably agreed upon by most of the readers of this book that such physical anthropomorphism can be

[1]This with some other data bearing on this subject I have cited in "Theology for Babes," *The Christian Century*, July 29, 1936.

attributed to God only in symbolic terms. There is no harm done by talking about the "everlasting arms" if one knows that this means protection and care rather than biceps. One may talk about abiding "under his wings" if this is not taken too literally. The injunction to labor "under the great task-master's eye" has been a wholesome incentive to faithful performance of duty, though outside of the hymns we do not use this terminology much in these days. The parents and religious education experts who bend over backward to teach children nothing about God, lest they pick up some anthropomorphic ideas, need to ask themselves whether a vacuum is more to be desired than meaningful symbolism.[2]

Yet, though physical traits can be ascribed to God only in picture language, there is less certainty about the extent to which *psychical* traits can be attributed to deity. Are love and a correlative wrath against evil, watchfulness, forgiveness, mercy and kindness, all of which are familiar human emotions, to be taken as literally descriptive of the nature of God? Here we enter upon dangerous ground; for to say no is to run counter to long established Christian belief, while to answer in the affirmative is to expose oneself to the charge of merely carrying one's anthropomorphism into less obvious forms than that of the person who gives God eyes and hands. Instead of saying either yes or no, we had better say, "Let us see."

The way through the dilemma seems to me to lie in

---

[2]It is a curious fact that the more "enlightened" parents give sex instruction to their children early in order to prevent their picking up wrong ideas from the environment; yet they reverse the process in regard to religion.

further analysis of what we mean by such psychical traits. As behavior patterns, the product of conditioned reflexes, we cannot attribute them to God without giving him a body, and as they manifest themselves in us human beings they are in part the product of the social conditioning of a biological organism. But as I tried to point out in Chapters III and IV, they are never wholly this. They are a super-physical expression of the highest reaches of personality. In an important sense they are also an expression of divinity. Such divinity, manifesting itself in self-direction toward ways of moral excellence, is a feeble glow in the best of us, though it shone full-orbed in the personality of Jesus. The power to envisage high goals and work toward their achievement may well be taken as descriptive of the essential nature of God.

If this be true, God is personal, with moral traits akin to ours, but so much more personal than we that it is necessary to be cautious about attributing to him our human traits. Note that I do not say, as is often said, that God is "superpersonal." To use this term is to say something meaningless, for while there might be something higher than personality we have no idea of what it could be. When I say that God is so much more personal than we that we must beware of ascribing to him human traits, I mean that he is like us in the highest characteristics of spirit of which we have any knowledge. These highest characteristics are the power of moral self-direction, rational discernment and control, creativity, the capacity to love persons, to love beauty, to strive for the achievement of greater values in our total social life. There is no incongruity in ascribing to God these characteristics if one has earned the right to do so by a survey of the total picture which the universe presents. Obviously, such natural human impulses as those of selfish acquisitiveness, pugnacity and sex cannot be ascribed to God without blaspheming him. But in the more-than-natural, transcendent element by which we hold these impulses in check and redirect them toward a greater good, it is appropriate to say that human nature is akin to the divine.

Are we, then, simply making God in our own image, as the humanists have often charged? It depends on whether the question refers to *reality*, or to our *knowledge of reality*. Epistemologically, we have no other route to travel except the route which begins in human experience. From what we know about man, viewed broadly, we must infer what we can about God. Some analogical reasoning is legitimate, provided we know where to draw the line against pushing the analogy beyond the evidence. Yet our knowledge could not go from man to God unless creation were from God to man. Metaphysically, God has made man akin to himself. There are many elaborate ways of saying this, dressed up in much verbiage, but I do not know of a better way than Genesis 1:27, "And God created man in his own image, in the image of God created he him."

I believe we need to be careful about diction at this point. To say "God is a person" is to invite men to conceive God in their image, as a sort of super-man. To say "God is personal" is to make personality a sign-post toward his nature. It is possible without sacrilege to ascribe to God man's highest traits and call him personal. But we must never say we know all about him. We might better say, as Professor Wieman does in picture language:

Here, not far away, are the brown foothills. These we know in their specific nature. We can see the masses of rock, the angles and slopes, even the trees. But beyond the foothills and higher, are the blue mountains. There the outline begins to fade. We cannot see the contours nearly so well. We know that the mountains are there. We know their reality as surely as we know the foothills; but we do not know their specific nature so well as we know the lower levels. On beyond the blue mountains, and higher still, are the purple heights of the loftiest and most distant mountains. There we lose entirely our vision of the contour and structure. We know those mountains really are there. Also we know they must have a structure. But what it is, we do not know, even while we know quite without doubt the reality of the mountains.[3]

2. IS GOD A FORCE?

If the foregoing be accepted, it follows *that God cannot be described in terms of any impersonal cosmic force.* The most common concept of God among college students is of a power that holds the world together and keeps everything in nature running smoothly. This is often vaguely deistic—a something-or-other that started things—but whether its operation is put back in the beginning or spread through contemporary existence, it is thought of as doing nothing except to cause things to be.

---

[3]"God Is More Than We Can Think," in *Christendom*, Spring, 1936. Some points at which I disagree with Professor Wieman will be mentioned later in this chapter.

Students often say that they can believe in that kind of God readily enough on scientific grounds, but they see no reason for supposing that God is personal. By personal they mean either "possessing the traits of personality" or, more often, "having a personal interest in me."

Close upon the heels of the statement that it is easy enough to believe in God as an impersonal force comes usually, "But it leaves me cold—" Students are seldom analytical enough to know why, but they know that such an idea is religiously ineffective even when intellectually acceptable. Some regret the slipping away of a warmer concept; some feel emancipated.

If we are going to deal fairly with this attitude we must see what there is in it. In particular, we must ask about the relation of "what runs the universe" to personality in both senses: that is, as an expression of personal traits, and as an agency of personal interest in human individuals. Let us look at each question separately.

If personality be taken to have as its most distinctive trait an ideal-forming tendency by which to overcome the limitations of human and physical nature, this clearly signifies both a rational mind and a concern for values. The evidences from science and the moral imperative mentioned in the previous chapter converge toward the belief that both *rationality,* manifest in the world's orderliness, and *moral concern,* manifest in the presence and increasing emergence of values, are characteristics of whatever Power it is that runs the universe. Grant that the world is "put together mind-wise" and has moral values at its center, and one must grant that this Power cannot be less than personal, however much more it may be. Nowhere else but in minds, and nowhere else in the whole field of sentient and conscious life but in personal minds, do we find the power to create and control through rational order and moral concern.

But what of the interest of this Power in us? In the vast indifference, so the argument runs, what place has man or his little day? Granting that this Power may have some interest in the development of the human race, what concern could it possibly have for *me*, an insignificant and tiny fragment of the whole?

To this argument it may be replied that it is based on that very anthropomorphism from which the believer in an impersonal deity desires to flee. No human being, certainly, could have a personal interest in and grant personal aid to every person on the continent of Asia—to say nothing of the planet as a whole, and possibly Mars besides! But neither could any human being create and sustain the universe. Whatever Power it is that keeps the stars and atoms swinging in their orbits must either be infinite or so far beyond man in power that it is bootless to place upon him human limitations. If God can keep the stars and atoms swinging, there is a barrier only in imagination, not in reason, to supposing that he can have concern for me.

Another answer is that if God be thought of in scientific terms, as immanent energy pervading every part of the universe, this does not remove him from within us. For if he (or it) is in all nature, this Power is also within that part of nature comprising our physical bodies. Our bodies are the most intimate part of the environment in which our personalities have their being. It then becomes literally true, in Tennyson's words, that "closer is He than breathing, and nearer than hands and feet." Such presence does not necessarily imply spiritual awareness: but it makes credible the possibility of the spiritual presence within us of that Power which sustains the universe. It is a grave mistake, made sometimes by religious leaders who ought to know better, to assume that the deity one reaches by way of mathematical physics is all we need— a substitute for the God of personal communion. Such argument, however, is valid as far as it goes, and useful in breaking down the sense of remoteness which leaves the God of personal communion behind a veil of impersonality.

3. IS GOD NATURE?

In the third place, *God is not the whole of nature, nor any part of it.* To prevent misunderstanding I must say immediately that I do not deny the divine immanence in both physical and human nature. In fact, a large part of the argument hitherto has rested upon evidence that there is such immanence in the world. But to say that God is *in* the world is not to say God *is* the world.

God cannot be identified with nature as a whole. If you make him everything in general, you make him nothing in particular. There are other objections to pantheism, centering particularly in the assault to human freedom and the complications regarding the problems of evil and error if man loses his identity in God. But the basic objection to pantheism is that if we have a *deus sive natura,* a God = nature, we might as well—as far as any logical considerations carry us—take the second part of the equation and let the first part go. This is what happens when a great pantheism, like Spinoza's, originally sustained by religious vitality and insight, loses its vision of God to pass over into atheistic naturalism. The opposite happens in Hindu mysticism where nature is rejected as illusion and God is retained as sole reality.

God is not the whole of nature. Nor is he *any part of nature.* By this I mean that he is not a thing among other things, nor one center of activity among many activities. If he were an object in the space-time order it would be possible to discern him by telescopes and microscopes and measure him by meter-sticks. No theist holds this to be possible. Though "all the choir of heaven and furniture of the earth, in a word all those bodies which compose the mighty frame of the world,"[4] may give evidence of his immanent presence, this is quite different from saying that these are God.

The problem is somewhat more difficult with reference to human nature. Is not God that part of me which makes me live triumphantly, if I do? The answer turns on the meaning given to "part." Certainly, God is no fragment of me, as if a human personality could be dismembered. As God is immanent within all physical nature, manifesting himself as creative energy everywhere but as a God of values in some things more than others, so is God immanent within all human nature as the sus-

[4]Berkeley, *Treatise Concerning the Principles of Human Knowledge,* §6.

taining source of man's existence, the impulse to man's most creative effort and his most satisfying peace. With due care to avoid spiritual pride, a man may say that God works *through* him, *with* him, *in* him.

But at no point may a human being surrender his own freedom to merge his identity in God. God creates us, but he maintains no "absolute sovereignty" over us or in us. When I do my work, even with the best of God-given strength, it is *my* failure if I fail, *my* triumph—in a measure —if I succeed. Whatever increment of power comes to me from divine grace, I get through submitting myself to God and accepting God's reinforcement to my ordinary powers. I ought, because of this, to "give God the glory." But this is quite different from saying that God and I at some point merge our being.

With regard to both physical and human existence, it seems necessary, therefore, to say that God is no part of nature. Yet God is immanent in both, as he is also transcendent to both. An understanding of his relation is perhaps helped by an analogy centering in the primary thesis of this book. In human nature, as the capacity to live by ideals is immanent in and transcendent to our bodies, inseparable from them yet with a reality and a meaning not to be identified with any bodily structure, so in the divine nature is God's personality immanent in and transcendent to his entire created universe.

4. IS GOD A PROCESS?

God is not a process, nor a form of interaction. Some who would say readily enough that God is neither the whole nor a part of nature in any sense which would make God a substance nevertheless maintain that he is a form of activity, or process, within nature. This, if I am not mistaken, is what Professor Wieman means when he defines God as an interaction, as the structural integration of values, or as growth in meaning and value.[5]

My admiration for Professor Wieman as a man of religious vision is very great. His position is difficult for orthodox theists to accept, at least partly for the reason that his sense of God's greatness makes him unwilling to confine God within conventional categories. However, I find intellectual, practical, and historical difficulties in his view.

First, there is the intellectual difficulty that an interaction or process—even so vital a process as growth in meaning and value—is both too narrow and too broad a term by which to describe God.

It is too narrow because it implies order without an Orderer, agency without an Agent. The point at issue, of course, is whether an Orderer or Agent is essential to order and action. Quite conceivably there might be some kinds of action and change without a personal agent. Yet the reason why Professor Wieman (or any one of similar trend of thought) is a theist is precisely that it is not just any kind of action, but *inter*action, which the universe reveals; not mere juxtaposition but *orderly* arrangement; not mere change, but *growth* in meaning and value. This

[5] I discuss Professor Wieman's philosophy on the basis of his more recent affirmations. His earlier definition of God as "that upon which we depend for our greatest good" does not seem to me to connote a process.

146

suggests that to define God as a process—as something which happens—is to fail to say what makes it happen in this way.

On the other hand, interaction is too broad a term to give definitive meaning. Professor Wieman, I believe, does not maintain that every interaction is God but that God is those interactions by which growth in meaning and value takes place. Even when interaction is given this limitation, it is still too broad a term to denote a concept which can properly be equated with God. To illustrate, the interaction of seed, soil, sun and moisture by which a tree grows is a process of growth in meaning and value. The oak *means* more, it is *worth* more than the acorn, not only in economic terms but by any criterion of beauty or utility one wishes to apply. But the oak is not God. Nor is the process of its growth. Nor is the total process of vegetative life of which it is a type. Both the product and the process may well be the work of God and a manifestation of God's agency. "Only God can make a tree." But whether a poet or a metaphysician says it, it is one thing to say that God makes a tree by his immanent activity in nature, and another thing to say that God is the way a tree is made. If God is an interaction in the latter sense, divinity gets spread so broad that it becomes too thin to carry a distinctive religious meaning.

A fairer and more pertinent illustration might be some form of human interaction, such as friendship, mutuality, or "community"—about which much current discussion centers. If God is not to be identified with processes of vegetative growth, is he human love, expanding social justice, "birth in beauty"? At this point Professor Wieman, theist though he indubitably is, adopts a position which shares some of the limitations of humanism.[6] If God is identified with any human aspiration or achievement, even though of the most glorious type, we have human nature functioning highly—but where is God? Just as an identification of God with physical nature passes over into naturalistic atheism when the glow of religious vision cools, so the identification of God with any human mutuality tends to leave us social ideals but no more-than-human power by which to make them operative.

This leads to a second type of difficulty I find in Professor Wieman's thought, less relevant to intellectual analysis than to the practical aspects of religious living. This is the difficulty of praying to an interaction, or to any process of growth. One might worship such a deity in the sense of feeling reverence for the creative processes of the universe. One might, in a somewhat less personal sense, praise it for being. One might try to act with it instead of in counter-currents. These are good things to do. But how worship of, praise to, or cooperation with an impersonal process could without intellectual inconsistency become *prayer* baffles me. I do not say that prayer on such a basis is impossible.[7] But to pray to a process is, it seems to me, impossible without the interpolation of a

---

[6]Professor Wieman is not a humanist, for he has a great sense of the superhuman forces which are at work within human life and in physical nature. My point is that these forces ought not to be identified with the interactions and processes of growth which they produce.

[7]Professor Wieman's *Methods of Private Religious Living* is the best book available on methods of worship.

concept of deity which goes beyond the terms of the definition.

In saying that prayer requires personality in one's deity, I do not mean by prayer simply petitions for changes in external events. I mean an approach to God for the strengthening of the inner life. Such prayer seems to me inevitably to imply an expectancy of response from a transcendent deity to give it meaning, and no such expectancy can be built with intellectual consistency upon the belief that God is an impersonal process or structure of meaning.

This carries me to a third point of difficulty in this concept of God—namely, a lack of recognition of the historical foundations of religion. It may well be that there are errors in the Biblical account of the way a personal, transcendent deity moved among men and revealed himself to them. Even the highest points of revelation in the Hebrew-Christian tradition—those through the prophets and Jesus—have to be read with discrimination. Yet these, with the further record of man's experience of God in Christ through nineteen centuries of Christian history, are indubitably *there*. To conceive of God in other than personal terms requires either a rejection of such records or so great a reinterpretation that the Christian heritage becomes in large measure unrecognizable. I do not say that we are unjustified in disregarding the past and "starting from scratch" if this will get us nearer the truth. A philosopher of religion is not obligated to become a theologian—in fact, he is obligated not to become one if by doing so the objectivity of his search for truth is blurred.

But when so much, both of the incentive to religious experience and the data upon which we must work in religious analysis, comes out of the historic past, to fail to incorporate this into the framework of belief is to miss part of the evidence.[8]

I have tried in this chapter to say some things about what God is not, as an avenue of approach to a more positive statement. I have said that God, though personal, is not a person in the ordinary sense of this term; that God is not an impersonal cosmic force; that God is not the whole of nature nor any part of nature, physical or human; that God is not a process in nature, though he is immanent in all nature as well as transcendent to it. In the next chapter these four denials will be countered by four affirmations.

[8]I have discussed Professor Wieman's position at some length, not simply because I disagree with him, but because he has presented a significant challenge to orthodox theism which is more influential in American religious thinking than any other trend of thought except liberal or "realistic" theology.

Chapter XII

WHAT GOD IS

By CONSIDERING what God is not, I trust we have cleared the ground somewhat for considering what God is.

I. WHAT GOD IS

No human mind can do more than touch the fringes of mystery at this point. "'The purple mountain mystery of his majesty" looms above and beyond us. But we can find trails that lead upward. These trails I find in four convictions which I shall first state as propositions, and shall then attempt briefly to develop.

These propositions are:

1. God is Organizing Mind.
2. God is the source and goal of ideals.
3. God is the Cosmic Companion.
4. God is the Poet of the universe.

a. God is Organizing Mind

By saying that God is Organizing Mind, I mean that the interacting orderliness of the universe, with its integrated structure of physical and chemical elements and its emergent levels of evolutionary development, points to the existence of a Mind with both a capacity and a concern for order as a dominant characteristic.

As was earlier suggested, this Divine Mind cannot be held to be just like ours. It has neither biological history nor physical limitation. It is completely active; our activity is but partial and diffuse. It is all-wise; our wisdom but "a torch of smoky pine." It is all-good; the goodness of even the best of us is full of inner corruption and external compromise. But this Mind can do, and on a scale of "grand strategy" does, what human minds do on a small scale. It creates; it initiates and directs meaningful activity; it has concern for goodness and moves toward ends; it brings what would otherwise be chaotic elements into system and order. The term mind is not a misnomer because *nothing else but a mind can do these things.* At least, nothing else we know of does them, and to assume that something else might, though it is within the bounds of theoretical possibility, is to leave certainty for supposition.

Although at some points to be noted later,[1] I do not wholly assent to Plato's theory of creation, I see no reason to set aside the essential meaning of these classic words from the *Timæus:*

Let me tell you then why the creator made this world of generation. He was good, and the good can never have any jealousy of anything. And being free from jealousy, he desired that all things should be as like himself as they could be. This is in the truest sense the origin of creation and of the world, as we shall do well in believing on the testimony of wise men: God desired that all things should be good and nothing bad, so far as this was attainable.

[1]Chapter XIII, sections 1 and 2.

Wherefore also finding the whole visible sphere not at rest, but moving in an irregular and disorderly fashion, out of disorder he brought order, considering that this was in every way better than the other.[2]

The words, "so far as this was attainable," are significant and suggest, I believe, a truth left out of the dominant Christian tradition which has assumed God's power to be wholly unlimited. God works with and through both man and nature to erect an ever-growing structure of meaning and value. This means that the world is still in part unfinished. Instead of throwing up one's hands—and one's religious faith—before this idea, one might better find a challenge in the thought of a dynamic God who is always doing things—a God who "worketh hitherto" and still works to bring order and richer meaning into his universe.

b. God is the source and goal of ideals

To say that God is the source and goal of ideals is to say that while all ideals have a socio-biological history, those which make for true goodness have also a cosmic foundation. While all ideals have an end to achieve in the temporal order—else they would not be ideals, our higher ideals point beyond it towards perfection. That in which such ideals are grounded, and the moral perfection to which they point, is God. God is both the source of the supremely worthful in human life and the object of supreme worth.

[2]Op. cit., 29, 30. Jowett's translation.

The question may—and must—be asked as to where the dividing-line lies between those ideals of which God is the source and those of which he is not—those which are pointers toward his perfection and those which are subtle rationalizations of our own arrogance and pride. If man attempts to *be* God he sins the worst of sins, giving himself over to the soul-destroying selfishness of the will to power. If man attempts to *live like God,* to the limits of his wisdom and moral capacity, he finds all of life transformed into richness and power. He does not then attain moral perfection, but he does attain triumphant living. It is more than an academic question to know what ideals are of God.

So important is this question that later a fuller section will be devoted to it.[3] It may be said here, in anticipation, that God is the source of all biological and human life and therefore in one sense the source of all human ideals with their biological and physical matrix. As independent personalities, we form and act upon some ideals which are good, some which are evil, some which do not seem to make much difference. Yet in a moral sense, God can be thought to be the source and goal only of those ideals which, viewed most inclusively, are seen to enhance the values of life. We have noted how the evidence of history substantiates the judgment that there are eternal moral principles written into the structure of the universe to be thwarted at our peril.

As to which specific ideals do, and which do not enhance human values, inclusive judgment in the light of the

[3]Chapter XV, section 1.

154

supreme worth of personality must be the arbiter. Fortunately, no normal human being is wholly lacking in the intuitive and rational capacity by which to judge some things to be better than others. Where such judgment is mistaken, empirical study of factual circumstance and a union of reason with love is the corrective.

c. God is the Cosmic Companion

The climax of creativity, according to Professor Whitehead, is the love of God for the world whereby God becomes "the great companion—the fellow-sufferer who understands."[4] This is perhaps the profoundest insight of Christian faith, and one we could least afford to surrender if we had to give up any. It is also the one most open to self-deception, and to caricature.

I have no great admiration, either theologically or æsthetically, for that gospel song, the chorus of which affirms ecstatically:

And He walks with me, and He talks with me,
And He tells me I am His own,
And the joy we share as we tarry there,
None other has ever known.

Yet while I should never select this hymn for a service of worship over which I had any control, it affirms a deep-lying truth which is at least as much responsible for its popularity as are its sentimental words and lilting melody. When a person says or sings that Jesus walks by his side, he is of course speaking symbolically, and if he

[4]*Process and Reality,* p. 532.

did not *know* he were speaking in symbols he would be the victim of an hallucination, headed for a hospital for the insane. Fortunately, most of the people who sing this hymn are aware that Jesus does not literally walk and talk with them.

All deep emotion must speak in symbols. What is here symbolized is a sense of being not alone in the midst of a lonely world. One feels, and must describe somehow, the intimate Presence of a sustaining personality. This personality like the most satisfying human comradeship alleviates fear and confusion and gives moral support, yet unlike any human comradeship can be relied upon with implicit trust in the midst of any difficulty, however dark.

Whatever may be said of the psychological explanations of this assurance, metaphysically it does not rest upon illusion. God is that Power within the universe that enables us to feel within ourselves that we are not alone, that we have more than each other, that there is something objective and eternal to give us direction and leadership. There are many ways to say this, all falling short of the depth of meaning in which such confidence is grounded. One of the great historic ways of saying it is the Biblical figure of the pillar of cloud by day and the pillar of fire by night. If God's leadership today is by the clouds of the subconscious or the fires of imagination, this does not make such companionship less real.

d. God is the Poet of the universe

Of all the symbols by which we speak of God, the one most familiar is that of fatherhood. I have no desire to supplant it with a rival, fraught with meaning as it is through its familiar use by Jesus and many centuries of Christian testimony. Yet when the early creed-builders wrote "I believe in God the Father Almighty," they immediately had to add "Maker of heaven and earth." A Latin word for maker is *poeta*,[5] and it seems not inappropriate to speak of God as the Poet of the universe. God does what a poet must do.

What must a poet do? At least five things mark off the work of a poet from that of a rhymster. (1) A poet must create something, and the thing he creates must be both a mechanism and an organism. That is, it must conform to definite requirements of interrelated structure, a structure not only related part to part, but part to whole. (2) The created work must possess beauty, with a unity and symmetry of form in which the form is the inconspicuous but essential vehicle for the conveying of a meaning to which it is appropriate. (3) The poem must say something worth saying. The meaning must not be too obvious. The poem must not too plainly point a moral. But it must make its contribution to the richness of life. (4) What the poet creates must say something which comes from his own personality as a revelation of its nature, yet projects itself outward to meet a response in other minds. Only appreciative minds can make this response. (5) The poem must possess universality of meaning. It may delight the senses, or intrigue the fancy, or rend the heart, but a real poem must somehow touch the deeper emotions and leave the hearer or reader with

[5]From the Greek ποιητής.

a sense of having been lifted out of himself, and upward, by a miracle of beauty.

All these things God does in his universe. We can call him Poet only in terms of symbol and analogy. It is to commit the logical fallacy of undistributed middle to make a syllogism and say:

> A poet creates—
> God creates—
> Therefore, God is a poet.

Yet we may keep within the bounds of logic and affirm that God creates a world of interrelated structure, of beauty of form, of oft-hidden but majestically discernible meaning, of self-revelation to kindred minds, of eternal significance which lifts the religious spirit upward and outward to new heights of goodness, truth, and beauty. If God does this, we are entitled to speak of him not only in terms of fatherly care but of artistic creativity.

2. GOD AND THE PROBLEM OF EVIL

Any one who has ever tried to write a poem knows that there are moments when the words, almost of themselves, shape themselves into symmetry and beauty; and there are other intervals, sometimes long arid stretches, when achievement is slight and *any* achievement is by pain and struggle. It is not inappropriate to suggest that something like this may be the experience of God in the making of his world.

The problem of evil divides into two interrelated parts, the problem of sin and the problem of suffering. Of

these the former is the more important, for it is worse
to sin than to suffer, harder to muster moral forces to
get rid of sin than to exercise intelligent caution to prevent suffering. Yet most people are more troubled over
the second than the first. In an intellectual analysis, it is
harder to reconcile a suffering world with a good God
than a sinning world. Leaving the problem of sin and
salvation for later treatment, we must inquire how to
fit the fact of suffering into the framework of belief
which has been stated as describing something of the
nature of God.

Most of the time-worn answers to the question, "Why
do the righteous suffer?" have a grain of truth in them—
or several grains—but not enough to fashion from them
a loaf of bread to nourish the spirit. Let us review them
rapidly.

An answer which was born of Zoroastrian parentage
before the Hebrews sat in exile by the waters of Babylon,
and which has persisted throughout Christian history, is
that the devil causes not only sin but all manner of calamity. It seems an easy explanation to relieve both God
and man of responsibility. But if we are going to believe the world a universe, this answer will not stand up
under scrutiny in any other than a figurative sense. There
cannot be, in one universe, two supreme contending powers. Whatever value Satan may have as a symbol of man's
sin or calamity or of nature's perversity, he can scarcely
be thought to *cause* these occurrences.

One of the earliest and most persistent answers to the
problem of evil is, "God sends suffering as punishment

for secret sin." This reply has tormented many righteous souls besides Job. Save in those cases where we can see a cause and effect relation between a transgression of moral law and its natural outcome, as in drunkenness and consequent disaster, or dishonesty and loss of public trust, this answer does not meet the facts. Too often it is the innocent bystander upon whom falls the weight of the disaster ensuing from sin. Drunken drivers kill other people at least as often as they kill themselves.

Another answer, hoary with age, is, "To test our faith." But would a good God smite an innocent child, dooming him to be crippled or disfigured for life, to test his faith? Or if it is the parents' faith thought to be under test, is not this an over-expensive method?

What is really implicit in the preceding is, "To deepen our faith." This stands on a much higher spiritual level, and it may well be that no finer response can be given than Job's "I had heard of thee by the hearing of the ear: but now mine eye seeth Thee." Yet this is an *attitude,* not an answer: and the hosts of maimed and thwarted lives which give no such response are a silent— or often an hysterical—witness that the issue cannot wholly be met upon this basis. There is too great a mass of unredeemed and unredemptive suffering in the world to make this all we need to say.

Traditional theology, of the Calvinistic strain, says in effect, "It is the will of a sovereign God. We cannot understand; we must not question His ways. That which happens is to be." Were this taken literally, it would cut the nerve of human endeavor to eliminate the causes of suffering. Fortunately it is not, for life is trusted more than logic at this point. What emerges from it is a value —namely, resignation in the face of inevitable disaster. This is a spiritual attitude of great worth, but it is not an intellectual answer to the question.

The answers of liberal theology come closer to the inner issues of the problem. They do not distort the nature of God into a Being who, if frankly described, could not be worshipped; and they do not, except by emphasis, obscure fact to save a theory. The argument runs, in general, like this: God, though in a true sense all-powerful, has voluntarily limited his power to create a world of human freedom and natural law. Man, in using this freedom, misuses it and brings disaster on himself and others. God, in willing the existence of a world of law, commits himself to the possibility that in its operation disasters may ensue. Yet freedom, an interrelated society, and law are blessings worth the price. It is man's duty to try to prevent suffering, relying upon an Almighty God for coöperation in the task. I believe this to be, in the main, a true answer, but not wholly adequate for reasons to be stated presently.[6]

Some voices have been raised within the precincts of philosophy and liberal theology to challenge frankly the belief that God is infinite in power. John Stuart Mill believed in a Finite God, saying that if God is infinite in power he does every day things that man would be hanged for doing. William James developed this view

[6]This view is stated more fully in my *Conflicts in Religious Thought*, Chap. IX. Since that was written I have changed my position somewhat.

further, and it is the main point of Professor Montague's "Promethean God" set forth in *Belief Unbound*.

Among these and others who have spoken for a Finite God, none has spoken with greater eloquence or clarity than my honored professor, Doctor Edgar S. Brightman. He maintains that the facts of existence negate the possibility that an all-good, all-powerful but voluntarily self-limited God is in control of the universe, and he defends the view that there is a recalcitrant Given within the nature of God which God himself must fight to overcome. The Given does not denote moral imperfection but limitation in the possibilities of action. God is a finite-infinite Being, finite in power but infinite in loyalty to reason and goodness, and in the capacity to make good come out of evil. This view has aroused much fruitful discussion. It has not gained very wide acceptance, for it seems to many to place a sort of stigma upon God and thus to prevent him from being the All-perfect object of devotion and trust.

The view which I shall present is not exactly like any of these. While a thoroughly satisfactory solution of the problem of evil is probably a hopeless quest, it seems to me possible to avoid some of the difficulties of these positions while preserving their contributions.

The usual liberal affirmation of the voluntary self-limitation of God in the creation of a world of human freedom and natural law may be accepted. But it is impossible without the glossing over of real evils permeating in scope and colossal in scale to explain all the pain, waste, and frustration of existence upon this basis. In addition to

God's self-limitation through human freedom and the orderliness of nature, perhaps God is limited by elements of recalcitrance in nature itself and by chance in events. If so, God and man must work together to overcome such limitation, with the prospect of much frustration as well as victory in the process.

One who holds to a personalistic philosophy is obliged to place all recalcitrance either within human persons or the Divine Person. Hence to Doctor Brightman the Given is within the nature of God. But if persons are not the only metaphysical realities, the opposition may come from another source. It is then "given" both in the divine nature and in the structure of the universe that some things should happen which God does not will to have happen. To explain what this means it will be necessary to state wherein I dissent from personalism regarding the concept of physical nature. This will carry us into another chapter and will make clearer a theory of evil at which I have thus far only hinted.

It is, perhaps, sufficient to say here that if God is really organizing mind, source and goal of ideals, cosmic companion and poet of the universe, he is a God whose wisdom, goodness, sustaining care and creativity transcend our power to think. Before such a deity we may bow in reverence, or rise in action, but so great is he that we shall never encompass his meaning to confine it within our grasp.

Chapter XIII

HOW GOD IS LIMITED

It is seldom that philosophers of religion take the trouble to explain what they mean by nature. Even philosophers whose interests do not lead them into religion are more often concerned with epistemological questions as to how to know nature than with what is to be known. It is imperative if we are not to fall into all sorts of loose thinking about the relation of the physical world to God to try to state what we are talking about when we mention it. This calls, in turn, for further statement of what is real.

1. WHAT IS REAL?

I was reared in the personalistic tradition which holds that God and human persons are the only metaphysical realities. Such a view does not, of course, make physical nature an illusion. It makes physical things the acts of God. That is, it regards nature as an eternal system of divine activity; not something God has created, or still creates, but something God *causes* with consistent regularity. Human persons, being relatively independent real units of existence, are created; physical things are caused.

To this view I still assent in part, but only partially.

My present view comes closer to a form of theistic realism. I now see no valid sense in which it is possible to say that only persons are metaphysically real. Only persons initiate intelligent activity, have rational apprehension of the world, act freely, or are governed by ideals. But it is to beg the question to say that anything which does not possess such ultimate causal activity lacks metaphysical reality. There are at least three other types of interrelated reality: events, things (living or inanimate), and eternal forms.[1]

An event, as the word suggests, is anything which happens. The world is full of events which can readily enough be called events by anybody.

> Hurricanes and fierce tornadoes,
> Wars and deeds of desperadoes,

also soft spring breezes, peace, and high-minded effort for social reform—these and other things quite too numerous to mention are events which actually happen, which make a difference in human affairs because they happen, and which vary greatly both in importance and moral quality. The point which is here significant is not the obvious fact that events do happen, or the more disputable but very important question as to which ones ought to happen. Rather, it is that events have a reality which is in part independent of the agent causing them.

To illustrate, suppose one makes a speech. This is a

[1]Ideas and ideals are real, but not as separate types. They are combinations of event and form: that is, psychological events and universal structures of meaning.

"real event"—whether a good speech or not—which would not take place without the activity of an agent. In one sense, then, the speech is dependent on the speaker. It expresses some aspects of his personality, and therefore partakes of his nature. But any one who has ever made his choicest address, only to find it garbled and distorted beyond recognition in next morning's paper, knows that speeches have a way of doing surprising things. This is because they have a reality which is not dependent on the speaker only but on the total set of circumstances, among which the previous thought patterns of the hearers and the physical environment are among the most important. All human activities, dependent on their agents though they are, have some measure of independence from the agent. Even such subjective but psychologically real events as fantasy and illusion owe their nature in part to combinations of circumstance in which past experience in a social milieu and present physical stimuli give rise to new associations of ideas.

The relevance of this fact to the problem of evil we shall presently state more fully. In anticipation it may be said that events which are "acts of God" are not uncaused; but neither are they necessarily occurrences in which everything happens as God would have it. It may be that God also is limited by circumstance.

But events in the sense of overt happenings are not the only events there are. Mathematical physics has demonstrated something which has to be taken on authority by most of us, but which there is no good reason to doubt: namely, that *physical objects also are events*. That is, they are systems of electronic activity. There is one kind of activity by which your eyes move to read what is written on this page; there is another kind which is the page itself. The page exists because a vastly complicated, invisible, but mathematically calculable, system of electrical energy is in operation. Professor Whitehead, in spite of introducing confusion into philosophical terminology, has rendered much service by showing that from the standpoint of modern physics any "actual entity" can just as well be called an "actual occasion."

What this does to physical things is not to dissolve their reality, but to reinterpret it. As much as one likes, one may describe an apple-tree in terms of moving electrons rather than matter, and still the tree *to our experience* remains a tree, and the apples which grow on it remain apples to eat and not merely to make computations about. The tree is a thing of beauty to look at—perhaps also a thing to climb into, to seek shelter under, or later to burn in the fireplace—certainly a thing from which in its prime to get apples which please our taste and nourish our bodies. In these experienced aspects, the tree is a real *thing,* not to be identified with, nor separated from, the system of real *events* comprising its inner structure. Likewise, as we shall note presently, if the tree is a manifestation of the activity of God, as the *experienced product* of that activity it has a meaning and function other than what it has in its correlative aspect as a *process* of activity.

But what of the reality of eternal forms? This is a problem which has teased the minds of philosophers from the time of Plato to the present, and this is not the place to review the history of controversy which has centered about their nature. Let us look again at the two illustrations cited above.

A speech, in so far as it makes any intelligible sense which another mind can grasp, embodies certain structures of meaning. The speaker composes his ideas; yet he *finds* them. The ingredients of his thought do not merely come to him out of the inheritance of social cultures. They have existed in these cultures and have survived to be passed on precisely because they were sharable ideas with a universal meaning to be appropriated by any mind rational enough to understand it.

The tree to which we referred also has certain structures which distinguish its nature, and make it something in particular instead of everything in general. Whether in its inner nature as electronic activity, or in its more observable qualities such as color, shape and texture, or in its value as a thing of beauty and usefulness, it is described in terms of certain recognizable characteristics. It might be other than it is, as it would be if it were a cherry instead of an apple tree; but we could not know it to be this tree *as it is*—like a cherry tree in bearing fruit but unlike it in bearing apples and not cherries—unless there were common forms and meanings by which to make the comparison.

Such forms—structures of meaning and value—must exist in minds or events or things. It is difficult to conceive how they could exist except in something which embodies them. Yet neither could minds, events or things exist in any sort of intelligible order unless they embodied the eternal forms,[2] which do not have to be made but *are*. Thus we are justified in asserting their reality, though it is reality integrated with the rest of existence and not in isolation from it.

2. GOD AND PHYSICAL NATURE

We are ready now to see what bearing this has upon the relation of God to physical nature.

It was earlier suggested that the physical universe is an integrated system, put together as only an organizing, unifying mind could make it. Viewed from the standpoint of its creation, the physical world is a complicated but marvelously interrelated system of processes. These processes in physical terms are pulsations of electrical energy; in metaphysical terms, the systematic activity of an organizing mind, the Poet of the universe, who labors to make his on-going world in conformity to eternal structures of meaning and value. The world *as created* is a process in which God has priority over the world in the sense that he makes the world and is not made by it. But this does not mean that God, at any point in time, created the world out of nothing. It seems more credible to think of the created universe as an eternal process—the never-beginning and never-ceasing activity of an immanent yet transcendent deity.

Yet the physical world *as apprehended* by us in our

2Professor Whitehead calls them *eternal objects* and declares that we must "seek the forms in the facts." Cf. *Process and Reality*, p. 30.

experience is not process primarily, but product. We see change everywhere, in the movement of waves, in the drifting of clouds, in "the gay motes that people the sunbeams." Some of these events seem to flicker and pass; from others we see relatively permanent results emerging, suddenly as in the falling of great rocks by which the contour of Niagara is·changed, gradually as in the weathering away of this rock. But for the most part, physical nature looks like a relatively finished system of created things rather than an unfinished system of creative processes. It is important to recognize that it is *both,* and that one aspect of its being is as real as the other.

In the creation of any tangible object, whether a physical universe or an object of human art, all four types of reality described above are present. They are *distinct, yet interrelated,* aspects of creation. Each of these has a meaning and significance not to be subsumed under any other.

This last statement is essential to an understanding of the theory of evil which I shall state presently. First, however, it may be well to show their relations by reference to a case of human creativity in which it will not be necessary to think about God or the inner structure of an atom.

A person writes a book. Neither the process of the writing, nor the written product, is identical with the writer. They manifest his purpose, and reveal much about him. He is responsible for writing as good a book as he can under the circumstances. But when the tangible created product passes from under his surveillance and is read by unappreciative persons, he cannot be held entirely responsible for the outcome.

Thus far we have three "reals"—person, event and thing; creator, process and product—entering into an act of creativity. But without the fourth the creation could not take place at all. A book could not be *written* by one person and *read* by another unless there were structures of meaning common to the minds of both, and common to all persons sufficiently instructed to have some idea of what it is about. In so far as what is written has sense, these structures of meaning are embodied in it. In so far as either author or reader understands the sense of what is written, he participates in their nature.

In the creation of a book, there is both order and spontaneity. Nobody writes a book except through the operation of certain definite mechanisms which it is the business of physics, physiology and psychology—perhaps even histology and bio-chemistry—to understand and describe. Yet a book of which the writing was wholly mechanical would not be worth writing—and still less worth reading. It is the spontaneity of the author's insights and his nuances of thought and expression which give the book its meaning and charm. Another kind of spontaneity, the accident of circumstance such as a chance conversation or a periodical dipped into while the writing was on, may give it a turn for better or worse.

Spontaneity, then, may express itself either in intelligent purposeful creation or in chance variations. Both kinds are usually present, though it makes a big difference in outcome which is dominant. Both kinds of spontaneity exist within the book's orderly system; neither kind can be reduced to order and explained away.

Let us get back now to God and physical nature. The analogy fails in one aspect, that the human author has his physical materials given him to work on, while God creates his materials.[3] This is important enough so that it needs to be held in mind to avoid befuddling the argument. But at the points which bear on the four types of reality and their interrelations, the analogy holds. God (the creator) creates the physical world (the product) through his intelligent purposeful activity (the process), and it has meaning for our minds because he uses eternal, universal structures of meaning (forms) in its creation.[4] All are interrelated, but neither creator, product, process nor form is to be identified with any other.

The physical world, as created by God, is both something which happens and something which is. In human creativity, the process of creating a book is readily distinguishable from the book which is the created product. It is at this point that the distinction between the human author's making his book out of materials given him and God's making his own materials becomes relevant. Yet even in God's creating, there is not real identity of process and product; for as I have tried to show, the physical world as it is being eternally created (a system of events) is not identical in experienced meaning with the world

---

[3]It is at this point that Christian cosmology diverges most sharply from that of Plato.

[4]*Form* is the necessary condition of any orderly creation: the specific *forms* which enter into the process of creation might be other than they are.

as potentially or actually apprehended (a system of things).

This is not to say that one thing is two things—one of them a process and the other a product. Nor that a product is just a way men have of looking at a process. Rather, a physical thing as the product of God's creative activity means something and does something which it does not mean or do as a process of that activity. This is because it exists in an interrelated world—with relations which extend not only to God who creates it and men who perceive it, but to very many other things in a very intricate structure of events.

What all this means in terms of a specific physical object, like a cherry-tree,[5] is that it exists as the product of a process of electronic activity functioning according to the agency of Mind in an interrelated system. As perceived or thought about by human minds, it is distinguishable from other physical objects by the fact that it contains within itself certain combinations of form—that is, certain qualities and characteristics—which other objects unlike it do not possess. It comes to have these qualities through existing in an ordered system, within which there is both intelligent purpose and chance. Sometimes human order and spontaneity enter in to determine its nature, as in any manufactured thing or product of human art; sometimes not. But there is always *both order and spontaneity* present in its creation.

This means, in brief, that physical nature is the deriva-

[5] I choose Berkeley's famous example, not because I agree with his view, but because in certain important respects I do not.

tive product of Mind, event and form; but also that it has a character of its own which though derived from these cannot be submerged in them. If this is clear, we are ready to take up the question of what it is that limits God.

3. WHAT LIMITS GOD

To ask, "What limits God?" is to imply that something limits him. To some minds it is sacrilege or presumption to raise the question. Is not God infinite in power, as in wisdom and goodness, the "absolute sovereign" of all our destinies?

To this the reply is that unless we are to refuse to open our eyes and look around us, we can scarcely say that everything in the world is the way a good God would want to have it. "From war's alarm and deadly pestilence" we may well ask God to save us, but there would be no point in asking God to save us from them if we thought God wanted them to happen. Though there is deep meaning in the Leibnizian phrase, "the best of all possible worlds," which is often missed by those who jeer at it, nobody without optimistic myopia could take seriously the idea that the world, just as it is, is just the way it ought to be.

What then prevents the world, with its destinies controlled by a good God, from being what it ought to be?

The first answer, and it is a valid answer as far as it goes, is the voluntary self-limitation of God in the creation of a world of human freedom and orderly natural law. This answer is valid *unless it is made to go too far.* It often has been.

174

There seems to me to be no adequate way of dealing with the problem of human sin, with its resultant sequence of outer calamity and inner dissolution, unless it is recognized that man has some measure of freedom of choice. What happens when freedom is denied is the wholesale elimination of a sense of sin. But while sin may thus be theoretically ejected, it stays by us nevertheless, even more potent in its hold from the fact that "if we say that we have no sin, we deceive ourselves." The problem is met, theoretically, a great deal more satisfactorily by admitting without blinking both the fact of sin and the heinousness of sin, and saying that God created us with the power to do evil in order that we might have the power to choose to do good. To have the power to *choose* our goodness instead of having it thrust upon us is God's greatest gift to man, and by it God limits himself.

I have suggested that God works in the physical world by a procedure in which there is both order and spontaneity—regularity of functioning and teleological creative advance. This is another way in which God limits himself. Though the orderliness of nature and the progressiveness of evolutionary development as a whole may be conceived to be God's will, some things that happen in them can be held to be so only in the general sense that God has willed that there be a world in which, for the greater good, regularity at some points may thwart value.

To say that God has voluntarily limited his power by the creation of a world of human freedom and natural law is only to say what liberal theism has long said. God is still in an important sense omnipotent if all that limits him is something which happens within his purpose. It is important here to distinguish between what he purposes in the kind of world he has made, and what he wills in specific instances. To cite a familiar analogy, as parents for the sake of letting initiative be developed in their children may permit them to act as they would prefer them not to act, so God to fulfil the conditions of a larger purpose may *permit* a frustration of value which he does not *will*.

However, there is within the world process more of the kind of spontaneity which crushes value than can credibly be set down to voluntary self-limitation on the part of God. God is limited by *inertia in things* and *chance in events*. What these terms mean I shall defer saying for a moment. It is best to get at their meaning through illustration.

Death is the most inevitable necessity of life. It may be a blessing, or a stark tragedy. For creative advance, death is a biological necessity in order that the earth may be cleared of organisms that have had their day. Without it, the on-going currents of new life would have no opportunity. In individual experience, quite apart from its racial value, death in senility is a blessing. When powers have failed and the spirit, "clogged with the pollutions of mortality" has no longer richness to give to the world or get from it, it is better that death cut off the struggle. In such instances, there is no blasphemy in saying that what happens is God's will.

However, the real problem of evil emerges in the fact that not all death is of this sort. In fact, the greater part of it is not. Death in infancy with life as yet unlived, or death in maturity with function unfilled and rich values yet to be achieved, is tragedy. Violent death may be fitted into a sequence of cause and effect relations, but hardly into a concept of the will of a good God. Gloss it over as we may by saying that something worse might have happened, the fact remains that by any canons of judgment we know such premature or violent death ought not to have come *then* or *in that way*. If any person faced by bereavement of this type finds comfort in believing that God wills it so, I should hesitate to rob him of this comfort. Yet it is an illogical comfort, and there are securer foundations on which to build a structure of life's meaning in the face of desolation.

For the occurrence of death as a biological necessity, the system of nature provides adequate mechanisms. These we may legitimately say are God-given. But in their operation, these mechanisms do not act with due concern for values. There is an element of "cosmic drag" —almost as if nature were telling us not to set too high a store by our cherished dreams, an element of fickleness that invades our best-laid plans and brings them to apparent nothingness, an element of spontaneity that by no means works invariably for intelligent advance but seems, like the rain, to fall on just and unjust, and like the lightning, to strike at random.

The operation of such forces, apparently illogical and unconcerned as to what they smash, is most visible in the human realm where values are most precious. But it is not limited to the human. In the premature, violent death of even the lower forms of animal life, the will of

God is thwarted. We should take the problem of evil much more seriously than we ordinarily do if we faced with due concern the weight of unmitigated misery in the animal world. A clear-thinking philosopher who can scarcely be accused of sentimentalism has written:

It is not, however, the pains of the conquering strong that call for our pity, but rather the pains of the utterly vanquished and crushed. Pains, for example, of small rabbits delivered as playthings to young eagles or fox pups by their mothers to be nibbled, gnawed, or pecked at slowly; toads beneath the harrow, cats beneath the wheels of our cars, or captured mice in the claws of those same cats. For such pains there is no compensating heroism, no high religion or philosophy to snatch victory from defeat—nothing but writhing and screaming, trembling, terror, and despair.

There is an old, mean piety that would justify the ways of God at any price, even at the price of conscience, pity and sincerity. Contemptuously disregardful of all animal suffering, such piety concentrates on those few cases in which human pain can cancel human sin or hang a moral to a tale. There are such cases, but they make so small an islet in the seas of nature's agony that one needs must have the mind of a fool and a heart much worse to treat them as "solving the problem of evil" and freeing from blame a supposedly omnipotent creator. The puzzled, mounting wretchedness of a single dog lost on the streets of a city would be enough to damn with shame any God who ever lived in heaven if with omnipotence to draw upon he had ordained it so.[6]

It is this haphazard, undirected, often cruel spontaneity

[6]William P. Montague, "Philosophy as Vision," *International Journal of Ethics*, October, 1933.

which constitutes inertia in things and chance in events. By inertia I do not mean merely the bare fact that things do not move until they are moved. I mean, rather, that things have no concern for values and therefore do not "bestir themselves" to advance them. Such inertia is as evident in the destruction which falls swift and sure as in lingering torture. It is as manifest when things move too much as when they do not move at all.

By chance I do not mean any deviation from the orderly system of nature. In what we call an accident, physical forces keep functioning in their regular way, sometimes in intersection with human freedom as in most automobile accidents, sometimes quite apart from any human will as in earthquakes and landslides. Some of these accidents could be prevented by taking thought; some could not. Chance is present, however, in the fact that by no criterion of judgment which we should think of applying elsewhere can these particular juxtapositions of circumstance be held to be the manifestation of a system of values.

Our freedom, the regularity of nature, and our social interconnectedness whereby we participate in others' good as well as evil, are our greatest blessings. But this does not tell the whole story. As a human author's book has effects which he does not will because there are combinations of circumstance which he cannot control, so does nature have effects which God does not will and cannot control. There is a sturdy recalcitrance here, not a recalcitrance of free human beings who sin, not a recalcitrance of purposed regularities imposed by God upon himself, but the recalcitrance of inertia and chance.

Such inertia and chance God does not ordain, but struggles to overcome. The opposition is not to be placed wholly within his nature, for real things and real events present this opposition. This they do, not freely or maliciously, but because they lack freedom and know naught of either malice or good will.

What limits God? In part, human sin, ignorance and carelessness. In part, a God-given system of ordered and calculable nature which requires, for a greater good, that things happen as they do even though many things happen as neither God nor man would have them. In part, sheer inertia and sheer chance, woven into this structure of human opportunity and nature's dependability so inextricably that it is futile to attempt to say where one begins and the other ends.

If the foregoing statement is accepted, one must say frankly, without any hedging about to preserve a theoretical omnipotence, that there are actual limitations upon God's power. This means, from the standpoint of values and their achievement, a dualistic universe with conflict as a necessary element of its nature. But if what was said earlier in the chapter about the interrelatedness of persons, events, things, and forms be accepted, the universe is still a *uni*verse. It is not necessary to impute to things and events any freedom of their own, or to personalize them as a demonic power. By being what they are, in part inert and in part fortuitous, they oppose the advance of values and thus the will of God.[7]

[7]For further analysis see Appendix, p. 223.

4. WHAT GOD DOES IN TRAGEDY

Can we stop here, and say simply that disaster happens through inertia and chance and God can do nothing about it? By no means. To do so is to affront the great conviction of the Hebrew-Christian faith that "God is a very present help in trouble."

God is a present help in trouble precisely because "when the whole creation groaneth and travaileth in pain," God agonizes with it. To some minds the idea of a suffering God is repellent. Yet if there is one sure insight of the Christian Gospel, it is that the cross means something deep and permanent in the experience of God—a union of suffering love with spiritual triumph. It is the place where love and sorrow meet to make meaningful a crown.

What God can do in tragedy, and experience amply testifies that he does do, is to be "the great companion, the fellow-sufferer who understands." God is the source and goal of ideals by which to live triumphantly in the face of starkest grief. The sufferer who finds God as the strength and mainstay of his life does not merely acquiesce before the inevitable with stoic fortitude. He looks the tragedy in the face, and looks up to new heights of spiritual beauty to which he may mount by using his grief as a stairway to God's glory. The cosmic companion supports him with energizing power; the poet of the universe reveals to him insights hitherto unglimpsed. So led and imbued with power, the sufferer transcends his grief to become the suffering servant of humanity and to reincarnate in his own life the eternal meaning of the cross.

If God does this, he does the greatest thing which any deity could do. How he does it, we must subsequently examine. But if we view clear-eyed the fact that all is not in this world as God would have it, we must with equal clarity survey his agony and his redeeming power. God delivers us from evil; and to him belongs the kingdom and the power and the glory forever.

Chapter XIV

SIN AND SALVATION

BEFORE going forward it may be well to look back over the road traveled in the three preceding chapters. We have said that God is not a person in any popularly anthropomorphic sense, but in those higher attributes of personality whereby we transcend limitation to live sublimely, we are akin to God, and therefore he to us. God cannot be identified with any impersonal cosmic force, for if the universe reveals anything with certainty to scientific scrutiny it is order, and this requires an Ordering Mind as its source. Our sense of inability to feel personal communion with a cosmic deity is due in part to the placing of anthropomorphic limitations upon the scope of God's power, in part to failure to recognize that if he is in the stars of the heavens he must also be in our most intimate environment. God is neither the whole of nature, nor any part of it; and we found this to be true though in a somewhat different sense with regard to human as well as physical nature. We saw some reasons, intellectual, practical, and historical, for rejecting the view that God is a process of growth in value or an interaction between the component elements of the world of nature. Such negations led toward the conclusion that God is an ordering, value-loving deity, both immanent in the world and transcendent to it.

Asking then what God is, we found that we could not describe him with certainty but that there are pointers leading toward knowledge of him. Such knowledge as we may safely affirm was stated in four propositions: God is Organizing Mind, God is the Source and Goal of Ideals, God is the Cosmic Companion, and God is the Poet of the Universe. Such affirmations do not contradict the older, richer figure under which we have thought of God as Father, but they supplement its meaning.

This led us into an examination of the greatest barrier to belief in such a God, namely, the problem of evil. All the traditional explanations are unsatisfactory. The devil is not the source of disaster. God does not send it on the righteous as punishment for sin or to test our faith. It is to dodge the issue to say that suffering comes as the inscrutable and predestined act of a sovereign God, and the usual liberal interpretation in terms of voluntary self-limitation fails to reach to the heart of the matter. To assert simply that God is finite, or to posit the existence of a limiting Given—a racalcitrant element within God himself, is to deal realistically with the empirical facts of evil but to leave uncertain ground for the insights of religious experience.

An attempt at solution of the problem called for further examination of the nature of reality, and in particular the status of physical nature. It was affirmed that not only persons are real, but also events, things—whether living or inanimate, and eternal forms. Physical things are systems of electronic activity which in metaphysical terms may well be called the activity of God. But such activity, whether as process or product, is not identical with the agent; and things and events possess traits which cannot be subsumed under the will of God. These were described as inertia—or recalcitrant with reference to values—in things and chance in events.

Putting together the accepted insights of liberal theism regarding a God-given human freedom and system of natural law with this fact of inertia in things and chance in events, we find a world good on the whole, value-producing on the whole, but with disasters in it which God himself neither wills to have happen nor is able to prevent.

The conclusion was that this frank acceptance of limitation upon the power of God neither reduces him to a weakling nor affronts religious experience. On the contrary, God lends support which enables a man who avails himself of it to achieve spiritual triumph in any disaster, however dark, and from it to gain both insight and power for the better service of humanity. In the most worthful sense in which we can attach any meaning to the words, God delivers us from evil, and such a God merits our highest loyalty and devotion.

God delivers us from evil—this is evidently what God must do, if we are to live with creative idealism on the level of triumphant religion. But *what* does he do? What *can* we and what *must* we do ourselves in the process? What thwarts the work of redemption? And what responsibility, if any, have we for furthering the process in others? These are deep questions which we must try to probe in a concluding statement.

I. THE CHRISTIAN DOCTRINE OF MAN

It is necessary to go back to some things that were said in the third chapter, and restate them in the light of a doctrine of God which has now been stated but which at that stage it was not judicious to affirm, lest the case be prejudged.

We said that human nature is a mixture of original sin and original goodness, also of finitude and infinity. Left to follow the course most natural to us, our sin and finitude greatly overshadow our goodness and our transcendence of limitation. Partly through social conditioning, partly through self-directed effort, we achieve some measure of self-control and are able to regulate our lives by a non-coercive inner authority. That is, by the power of ideals.

This power of self-transcendence through the operation of a higher self we are now ready to call the spirit of God working within us, if we are careful not to fall into any pantheistic merging of identities. We must be cautious in more than one matter at this point. It is not true that every victory of ideals is the achievement of a consciously religious person, or that all our impulses to altruism can be glibly termed religious. The danger of such identification is to dilute religion to a point where it loses its distinctive nature to pass over into humanistic ethics. Yet whether we recognize the power of God or not, whether or not we deliberately attempt to mould our lives by his demands, he is still the under-girding foundation of our lives—the ultimate source of our higher ideals. The human function of religion is to make this *implicit* relationship become conscious and *explicit,* and thus more determining in our lives. If God works in us constantly this is not contrary to the belief—in fact, it reinforces the conviction—that as we consciously accept his presence and willingly work with him, we achieve vastly more of moral victory.

But is such acceptance essential to victorious living? Let us see.

In the moral enterprise, there is nothing which confronts the person of ethical sensitivity with greater force than the awareness that having done all that he can do, he is still an unprofitable servant. "The evil which I would not, that I do" is the perennial cry of the baffled spirit. The deeper one's spiritual and ethical insights, the more vivid the awareness of his shortcoming. Paul, with a keener knowledge of human nature than liberal theology has usually credited him with, saw this conflict and portrayed it in classic terms in the Epistle to the Romans.

In the latter part of the first chapter of this epistle is revealed a picture often passed over in preoccupation with the greater seventh chapter. Romans 1:19-32 appears to be directed toward the Greeks who knew God through the natural light of reason, but who were unable thereby to live much better than as if they had not had this knowledge. Paul speaks of the people who "knowing God, glorified him not as God, neither gave thanks; but became vain in their reasonings." Thereupon follows a terrific indictment of those who thought they could live good lives in self-sufficiency but whose acts proved that they could not. It requires little transcription to read in his words a vivid description of modern society with its self-righteousness, its glorification of man which passes over into bestiality, its lustfulness, creature-worship, sexual perversion, and all manner of evil. And not only do they describe the men of this time but of all times.

Seldom has there been brought together a more vitriolic list of words than Paul has assembled in the last verses of this chapter. They do not sound so bad when read in church in a "dim religious light" softened by stained glass windows, but exposed to the glare of day they sting and stab. Paul thus recounts the·achievements of those who try to live well apart from God's grace:

And even as they refused to have God in their knowledge, God gave them up unto a reprobate mind, to do those things which are not fitting; being filled with all unrighteousness, wickedness, covetousness, maliciousness; full of envy, murder, strife, deceit, malignity; whisperers, backbiters, hateful to God, insolent, haughty, boastful, inventors of evil things, disobedient to parents, without understanding, covenant-breakers, without natural affection, unmerciful: who, knowing the ordinance of God, that they that practise such things are worthy of death, not only do the same, but also consent with them that practise them.[1]

It has been the fashion in a theology over-tinctured

[1]Romans 1:28–82, American Standard Version. By permission International Council of Religious Education.

with the presuppositions of a secular psychology to smile at these words as the ravings of an over-morbid mind. But there is stark reality in them. Paul knew a great deal about psychology without using many labels.

Not only Paul, but Jesus, testifies to the fallibility and guilt which infest human nature. It is part of the greatness of Jesus that he saw people as they were and at the same time believed in them as they might be. The parable of the sower reminds us that seed is worth sowing even without great prospect of fruitage—but its optimism rests on the clear awareness that the seed which falls on good ground and brings forth thirty, sixty or an hundredfold is a very small percentage of all that is sown. "Strait is the gate and narrow is the way . . . and *few* there be that find it." The man who elicits Jesus' approval is not the Pharisee who thanks God he is not as other men, but the publican who calls himself the chief of sinners. It is because of "the hardness of men's hearts"—not the native goodness of human nature—that divorce is necessary. Repeatedly Jesus affirms a view of man which is equally realistic regarding man's actual evil and man's potential good.

The classical Christian tradition, following the lead of Jesus and Paul, has affirmed with remarkable unanimity the essential sinfulness and weakness of unregenerate human nature. Liberalism left the main stream when it capitulated to an over-romantic view, and it is well that Barthian theology is calling us back to it.

Yet along with an overwhelming sense of sin and futility there is found in the New Testament, in the great saints of Christian history, and in contemporary experience a paradoxical assurance of victory. It is the same man who cried out, "O wretched man that I am! who shall deliver me from the body of this death?" who says with calm assurance, "I can do all things through Christ." Even more significant is his word of victory over inner confusion and turmoil, "I have learned in whatsoever state I am, therein to be content."

I quoted a moment ago Paul's indictment against the sinfulness of the "natural," even the naturally enlightened, man. It is fitting to set in juxtaposition his paean of spiritual triumph:

Who shall separate us from the love of Christ? Shall tribulation, or anguish, or persecution, or famine, or nakedness, or peril, or sword? Even as it is written, For thy sake we are killed all the day long; we were accounted as sheep for the slaughter. Nay, in all these things we are more than conquerors through him that loved us. For I am persuaded, that neither death, nor life, nor angels, nor principalities, nor things present, nor things to come, nor powers, nor height, nor depth, nor any other creature, shall be able to separate us from the love of God, which is in Christ Jesus our Lord.[2]

Whence came this victory? There can be no answer save divine grace. In the midst of fear, loneliness, bewilderment, and over-mastering temptation there came peace and power. Living in Christ, one could look the world in the face, do a mighty work, and know that nothing could daunt the soul.

[2]Romans 8:35–39, American Standard Version. By permission International Council of Religious Education.

Translated into modern terminology this means that a tempted, frustrated life can find power through the power of God, and finding it can live on the level of triumphant religion. The God who is always the undergirding foundation of our ideals gives to these ideals, as we open our lives to let him, new direction, new depth, new breadth, new mastery. We live, then, by obedience to a non-coercive authority which is the authority not of self-interest, or of social conformity, or of entrenched habit, but is the authority of a Living Reality both objective to us and immanent within us. In obedience to this authority lies our peace, and our redemption.

2. THE MEANING OF SALVATION

The process above described is the essential meaning of what the Christian tradition has called salvation. The word salvation is not in good odor among large numbers of people, particularly young people, in our day. This is because it has often been associated with hysterical revivalism and other-worldly preaching. It connotes to many minds getting ready for heaven—and heaven is thought to be neither so certain nor so desirable as is the present life. To preserve the word salvation is not important. But to preserve what the word stands for is of supreme importance to individuals and to social groups.

The simplest and also the truest meaning of salvation is to take the word for what it says. In a lost, bewildered state one is saved from confusion and finds a sense of direction. In a tempted, frustrated state one is saved from defeat and finds victory through the power of God. In this process there is integration of personality, but salvation has in it a depth of meaning not found in such current terminology as "making a good personality adjustment."

Salvation need not—in fact, never does—come in a moment. One may grow into it through a lifetime. In the right kind of religious education, there need be no terrific crisis. Yet without some sort of personal awareness of the power of God in one's life and commitment to its obligations, salvation is a barren phrase.

3. WHAT MUST WE DO TO BE SAVED?

But what must we do to find salvation? Is it all done for us? Are some chosen to be saved and others lost? Manifestly not. The doctrine of predestination has largely passed out of modern thinking by the winnowing processes of history, and it is not probable that Barthian theology will effectively revive it. It too largely "goes against the grain" of our belief both in human freedom and God's respect for human personality. To say that man cannot save himself is a position both empirically and theologically defensible: to say that God saves men either contrary to, or in the absence of, human volition is to defy all that we know of human and divine nature.

To see what man does and what God does in the process of salvation it will be worth while to trace through the stages by which an individual comes into a vital experience of religion. These stages may be long drawn out, or compact together.

The first we shall call *awareness of need*. Theology has

192

traditionally called it "conviction of sin." It is this, but
in addition to a realization of one's sinful state comes also
a sense that the chaos and frustration of one's life require
a center of stability to be found in God alone. Desire to
be saved from chaos is no substitute for desire to be saved
from sin. Everybody would like to escape from the unhappiness of chaos; desire to flee our favorite sins is the
achievement of only a sensitized conscience. But from
both we need salvation.

This awareness of need must come through a stimulus,
usually the stimulus of the words or deeds of other human
persons. God works primarily, if not always, to save men
through human agents—a fact which places a sobering
responsibility upon those to whom Christian experience
is already vital. The stimulus may be a conversation, a
conference, a book, a service of worship, a public address,
or perhaps most often the impact of daily living. It may
be an emergency, when one is thrown back suddenly upon
his own strength, and finds he has none to stand on. Or
it may be a soul-racking decision which has to be made,
and one realizes that he has no center of light by which
to make it.

Through many centuries the Bible has been the most
important of all books—the record of the life of Jesus the
most important of all records—in stirring a sense of man's
need of God. If one's theology leads him to equate the
Christ of faith with the work of the Holy Spirit wherever
found, one may say that "there is no other name under
heaven whereby we must be saved." The Christian revelation, judged both by its foundations and its fruits, has in

it depths and heights not reached by any other faith. Tolerance becomes emptiness if one claims that all roads to God are of equal value. However, there is no justification for claiming that the Christian revelation, or the sense of direct personal relationship to Christ, is the *only* avenue which leads to God. In whatever manner comes the awareness of the need of divine resources, when the person to whom it comes responds to it and is ready to submit his will, God can work within him.

The second stage of the process, then, is *surrender*. Its relation to the first is stated with perfect psychological realism in the words of the parable of the prodigal son, "When he came to himself he said, 'I will arise and go to my father.'" What this means in living is that the person who thus surrenders gets a new focus of will. God moves from the periphery to the center of his consciousness, not dislodging awareness of self but transforming it by giving it new richness and new insights. With a heightened and deepened consciousness of self comes a new interest in other persons. What had been a limited and rather conventional altruism becomes a spontaneous, outgoing desire to further the good of others—not simply of the others close at hand but of those in wider circles where previously no claim was felt.

This shift in ethical focus necessarily involves repentance. Without it, there could be no surrender of self-will by which redemption could take place. The insights of historic Christianity have always linked forgiveness with divine grace, and have held repentance to be prerequisite to forgiveness. The church has not always known the reason why, but it is psychologically sound that there can be no redirection of will to channels of health until there has been a voluntary purge of that which was corrupting the soul.

The sense of forgiveness which comes with repentance does not mean that the sin which had a strangle-hold upon us vanishes away to be as if it had never been. The doctrine of forgiveness of sin means that when we genuinely become morally sensitive, with a new center of will which makes our former shallowness or baseness abhorrent to us, God gives new power to live in this new light. The battle is not yet won, and one of the most baneful distortions of Christian doctrine is that which assumes that when one is converted, all struggle with sin is over. The struggle remains, but there are reinforcements by which to win victories hitherto unachieved and often undesired.

The third step in salvation is *deliverance*. This is rooted in a paradoxical freedom. One surrenders his will to find his will reinforced with a power that he feels to be not his own. In his finiteness he feels himself to have infinite resources. Life takes on a new capacity to resist temptation, one finds amid confusion and bewilderment a new stability and center. Historic religion has made a great deal of this deliverance from sin, but we need equally to emphasize that deliverance is from impotence and turmoil.

The history of religious living is full of witnesses to this sense of release through self-surrender. If "conversion"—the turning about from self to God—seems an old-fashioned word connoting something not much to be desired, it is wholesome to remember that it has been the dominant motif of Christian history, and that through it unnumbered millions have found power. I do not say "found happiness," though that is there. One may do without happiness and find blessedness instead.

Such a deliverance comes through a paradox—one surrenders freedom to find freedom. Its greatest expression is in the words of Jesus, "Whosoever will save his life shall lose it: and whosoever will lose his life for my sake and the gospel's shall find it." Of the many citations which fill the records of all ages, one modern expression may be quoted which quite perfectly describes this paradoxical freedom. I choose it because it recognizes the need and the possibility of deliverance from finiteness as well as sin. This is George Matheson's familiar hymn:

> Make me a captive, Lord,
> And then I shall be free;
> Force me to render up my sword,
> And I shall conqueror be.
> I sink in life's alarms
> When by myself I stand;
> Imprison me within Thine arms
> And strong shall be my hand.
>
> My heart is weak and poor
> Until it master find;
> It has no spring of action sure—
> It varies with the wind.
> It cannot freely move,
> Till Thou hast wrought its chain;
> Enslave it with Thy matchless love,
> And deathless it shall reign.

In the first chapters of this book it was suggested that what is basically wrong with this generation—and in particular the younger part of this generation—is that

> It has no spring of action sure—
> It varies with the wind.

If this is a true analysis, and if divine resources are thus available, what our times need most is a resurgence of religion. There is needed a renewal of conviction that there are sources of stability which can be had only by paying the price of commitment.

In the Christian paradox of victory through surrender lies the way to personal power. Such power will not solve all the problems or cure all the ills of society. To suppose that it will do so without further effort is tragic error, or blasphemy. Yet without it the problems and ills of society cannot be solved or cured.

These are the steps by which one arrives at deliverance through surrender to a God "whose service is perfect freedom." But is it *perfect* freedom? Are there not barriers, both before and after the process of conversion, which sorely limit freedom? And what, if anything, can we do about them? This must be our next inquiry.

Chapter XV

BARRIERS TO RELIGIOUS LIVING

IT WAS suggested at the end of the preceding chapter that salvation, even though vouchsafed to man through divine grace, might not be easy to encompass. Revelation, whether of truth or power, is always a process which is incomplete until man appropriates what God offers.

The purpose of this chapter is to inquire what conditions within individuals and societies set barriers to living with creative idealism on the level of triumphant religion. It will be concerned with salvation, not in the specific sense of a conversion experience, but with the wider implications of religious living.

Three such barriers there are of very great seriousness, and any religious leader who either fails to see them or acts as if they did not exist does great harm. At least, to put it as charitably as possible, he fails to do the good he might. These barriers are (1) confusion as to what *is* the will of God, provided one wishes to do it, (2) thwarting forces in the environment which either greatly limit or make impossible victorious living, (3) barriers within ourselves. Each must have separate treatment.

1. WHAT IS THE WILL OF GOD?

A great deal of harm through all the centuries has been done by too blithe an assumption that we have only to desire sincerely to do the will of God, and we shall know what it is. Men have quoted, "If any man will do his will, he shall know of the doctrine," and without adequate consideration have then judged their own spontaneous promptings to be revealed truth. There is great meaning in this text—the meaning that right attitudes of will are essential to religious insights. But to assume that right attitudes of will are all that is necessary is to head towards the rocks. It is this assumption which makes fanatics; it is this which hallows the relative by giving it the sanction of absolute authority. This tendency to turn human judgments into divine commands makes religion one of the most dangerous forces in the world.

It is easy enough to see this fact when we look at religious cultures sufficiently far removed from our own. Mohammed thought he was doing the will of God when he took plural wives and sanctioned polygamy, and so presumably did Joseph Smith. The Jainists of India who will not take the life of an insect that spreads disease or a rodent that eats up the crops think they are doing the divine will. This is not limited to non-Christian faiths. Examples are written on almost every page of Christian history. The Inquisitors thought they were doing the will of God when they put heretics on the rack, as did Calvin when he caused Servetus to be burned at the stake. Doubtless most of the readers of this book are members of churches which owe their denominational origins to schisms caused by sincere disagreement as to what God desires his followers to believe and do.

We in our day have a naïve way of assuming that such persons were either sinful or unenlightened, implying that we in our superior goodness and wisdom should make no such mistakes. Yet the triple curses of modern society, racialism, nationalism, and economic exploitation, are shot through with rationalizations by which Christians still do horrible things in the name of God. One has only to dip into such books as Ray Abrams' *Preachers Present Arms* or Everett Clinchy's *All in the Name of God* to find plenty of evidence. A more fruitful though much more difficult course would be to search our own hearts and see what iniquity we find there.

What many Christian leaders do when confronted by this difficulty is to enjoin prayer and Bible reading as correctives. It is an important truth that prayer and the Scriptures are avenues to light. But it is a truth which becomes a dangerous falsehood when taken over-simply. One needs to pray in order to have his mind opened to new insights. One needs to read the Bible both for its devotional value and for what it shows of God's ways with men. One needs to act on the light one has in order to receive more. But none of these pursuits alone, nor all of them together, will rid us of the danger of putting in the focus of consciousness our own unrecognized and rationalized desires, or the cultural standards of our group, and sincerely believing that these are the will of God.

It is at this point very important to distinguish between, and the same time to bring together, the subjective and objective aspects of a moral choice. In any act there is both an inner motive and an outer consequence. No act is really good, however beneficial its results may turn out to be, if it proceeds from an evil will. For this reason self-interest, even an "enlightened self-interest," is never an adequate basis for morals. It skates too close to the edge of virtuous living, ready at any moment to topple over into the abyss of plain selfishness when social restraints are relaxed. But on the other hand, a virtue founded on good intentions only is a blind virtue which easily stumbles into ways of evil. The amount of damage done in the world by people who have "meant well" is incalculable.

The earlier part of this book emphasized the importance of ideals—that is, of motives—which for the best living must be both pure and potent. It is necessary to ask now how one may know whether his ideals are directed toward right ends.

As a corrective to an over-subjective, unbalanced virtue it is very essential to have, first, *an objective criterion of what is good,* and second, *a comprehensive and unbiased knowledge of the probable consequences of any projected act.*

Such a criterion of the good is found in inclusiveness of values as they contribute to the enrichment of personality. One does not need, unless he wishes, to go to religion for it. From the time of Socrates and Plato onward, the health and harmony of the soul has been a dominant ethical objective—called sometimes eudaemonism,[1] sometimes perfectionism, sometimes self-realization. It receives one of its most beautiful expressions in Socrates' prayer to Pan wherein Plato makes him say,

Give me beauty in the inward soul; and may the out-

[1]So called from Aristotle's *eudæmonia* which meant a combination of well-being and well-doing, happiness and virtue.

ward and inward man be at one. May I reckon the wise to be the wealthy, and may I have such a quantity of gold as a temperate man and he only can bear and carry.[2]

In modern ethical theory perhaps the most useful expression of this principle of the inclusiveness of values in a fully rounded life is Professor Everett's eight-fold classification of the values essential to personality. These, he says, are the economic, bodily, recreational, associational, character, æsthetic, intellectual and religious values.[3] The good life is that which, in integrated unity, embraces the widest possible range of these values. Since the selfish pursuit of these values automatically defeats the principle of inclusiveness, self-realization must necessarily involve the attempt to secure enrichment of life *for all*.

This approach is ethically valid. Whether or not one seeks a religious sanction for the good life, the enrichment of personality still stands as the major objective and criterion of goodness. There are other great theories, but they do not hold up so well under analysis. Hedonism is corrupted by the "hedonistic paradox" that the more one seeks happiness as an end in itself, the less he finds of it. It is unsatisfactory because of its exclusiveness; the person who seeks pleasure as a dominant ideal—even though pleasure be lifted to a high level—seeks something which may cut him off from fullness of life or lead him selfishly to deny fullness of life to others. A formalistic ethics like the Stoic or Kantian lays a most needed emphasis on purity of will, but is always in danger of failing to discern what values, in the total setting, one ought to try to advance.

[2]*Phædrus*, 279.　　　　　　　[3]*Moral Values*, Chap. VII.

The good will "like a jewel, would still shine by its light"[4] even if it were unable to accomplish its purpose, but it shines more clearly when centered upon worthy ends.

The principle of inclusiveness of values is no simple "rule of thumb," but it points toward greatness of individual and social living. If one wishes religious reinforcement for it, one finds it in Jesus' teaching of the abundant life. Respect for personality and the duty to make the values which enrich personality available for all men are the dominant notes in Christian ethics. These are written throughout the Gospels—in Jesus' concern for the poor, the outcast, the sinful, and the sorrowing; in his deeds of healing to body and soul; in his transcendence of racial and religious barriers to bring new life to a woman of Samaria or healing to a girl of Syro-Phœnicia; in his sending forth of disciples; in his own self-giving on the cross in loyalty to this mission. Examples need not be multiplied. We may safely say, on grounds both of reason and revelation, that to secure the most inclusive good for all people is the will of God for our lives.

But in a concrete issue, how apply this principle? Here we must bring into the picture what was stated above about the need of comprehensive and unbiased knowledge of the probable consequences of any projected act.

One knows, if he stops to think about it, that monogamy is better than polygamy, not simply because of the socially accepted standards of our group, but because monogamy makes for the permanence and sanctity of the home, the

4Kant, *Fundamental Principles of the Metaphysic of Morals,* Abbott's translation, p. 10.

spiritual equality of the wife, and the proper rearing of the children, in a way that polygamy does not. One knows that honesty is better than deception, because through deception social confidence is destroyed and both deceiver and deceived are harmed. One knows that to drink to the point of drunkenness is to lower one's physical, mental and economic efficiency, and one knows—if he is wise—that to drink moderately is the entering step towards drinking more than moderately. In the majority of issues which confront us, the principle of the more inclusive good, linked to a comprehensive judgment of the possible consequences, will make the way clear enough for practical moral living. *How* clear will depend on our breadth of judgment and keenness of insight.

But the way will not always be clear. Life is full of situations in which there are conflicting values, in which the probable consequences are only partially predictable, and in which such probable consequences as we can foresee will lead to an evil result *whichever course is chosen.* To cite again the matter of monogamy, just when in a particular case of serious incompatibility is divorce justifiable? And in time of economic stringency is a high-minded employer caught in the competitive system to cut wages and discharge men, or is he to let his business collapse from failure to balance the budget? In an international crisis are we to stand for collective security, or refuse to participate in anything that might lead to war? These questions suggest on the levels of personal, semi-personal, and larger group relations the utter complexity of the situation, and consequently the utter futility of claiming that the will of God for each of us is clear in all specific issues.

Living in the kind of world we do, the only thing we can do in these situations of conflicting values is *to do the best possible under the circumstances.* This "best possible" has to be judged by a wide survey of all the probable results. Having made the survey and formed the judgment, the thing to do is *to act,* undaunted by the awareness that the ideal is unattainable. It is better to attain it partially than through indecision or inertia to attain it not at all.

The question is often raised as to whether the ethics of Jesus presents an unattainable ideal. "Be ye therefore perfect, even as your Father which is in heaven is perfect," is a hard saying, and one life only has a record of such perfect moral purity that an injunction of this sort seems appropriately to proceed from it. Here again we need to remember the subjective and objective aspects of morality. Perfection of will is attainable to a degree that perfection of living is not. I do not say that any human being lives continuously with unstained good will. Even in our highest acts of moral and religious devotion there are subtle promptings to self-glorification. Yet to *will* the right is more possible than to *do* the right; and in spite of opposing circumstance or lack of knowledge by which to judge fully the consequences of action, some great spirits do achieve an active saintliness of character in which there is an almost perfect embodiment of Christian love. It is toward such purity, engendered in the inner life to flower in outward action, that the Christian ethic points.

We do the will of God when our wills are dominated by the ideal of love and when our acts are the best possible under the circumstances. In brief, we do God's will when from the best of intentions we do the best we can. But none can afford to say, prematurely or over-simply, that he has found and done his best. It is true to the nature of the Christian faith that those who do it best will be least ready to boast that they have found the way.

Such certainty as this affords, though it must be a certainty always open to revision, is of supreme importance. Confident that the "best possible" really is the best one can see to do under the circumstances, one can act with assurance of divine support. With eyes open to need of change in strategy and mind sensitive to learn from other minds, one can give himself to the task at hand. He can know that though the endeavor may end in temporary, or even in an earthly sense, in final defeat, still no good act is ever lost. History is long, and in the still longer vista of eternity God's way must triumph. With this flexible, yet adamantine, certainty one can face anything. Some great spirits have it, and thereby have achieved triumphant living.

But not all. Some cannot. What prevents?

2. OBJECTIVE BARRIERS

We said earlier that there were things outside of ourselves which set limits to our serving God with perfect freedom. To point to such obstacles as excuses for our own inactivity is pernicious; to see fairly how they limit other people is Christian—and indispensable both to charitable judgment and effective service.

Foremost among these barriers is the economic system. There is so much to say about this that I shall say but little. We live in a society wherein great numbers of persons have less than the minimum "daily bread" which is needed for effective personal living, while others have too much. Among the results are limitation throughout the whole range of values essential to personality, and in particular a limitation of freedom of opportunity under guise of maintenance of liberty; callousness, indifference to human need, and exploitation by those in power; bitterness among the exploited and a state of affairs in which violence readily begets violence; the harnessing of economic power to all our major institutions and their consequent control in defence of the *status quo*. In particular, schools and churches—the two institutions most responsible for imparting unbiased knowledge and inculcating ideals of respect for personality—must dance to the tune of those who pay the piper.

These results of the economic system in which we are forced to live have ramifications which reach to every human being, making us all its victims and involving us all in social sin. However honest we try to be in personal relations, we draw wages or salaries or dividends from sources which do not have to be traced far back to become involved in shade. If we do not sin otherwise, we sin at least by acquiescence. The fact that in general the underprivileged are the victims and the privileged members of society the aggressors should show us on which side of the class struggle to cast our effort. Yet this should not blind us to the fact that in some measure *every person* is both sinned against and sinning because of a profit-centered economic order.

The iniquities of our economic life touch all the other barriers which will be mentioned. It is easy for those who live in plenty to say that the spiritual life ought to rise above material things. In some measure it can; in another measure it cannot.

There is the matter of health, whether physical or mental. A birth injury may place upon a personality a permanent handicap which neither God nor man can overcome. If a child does not have the right nourishment before he is two years old, he may never have either the bone or the "back-bone" to live resolutely by exacting ideals.

Against the assumption that all sin is mere mental sickness, it is necessary to protest vigorously in the interest of maintaining both the truth and such shreds of will-power as a deterministic psychology has left us. Yet against indifference to the effects of moral limitation by physical or environmental handicaps, it is necessary to protest with equal vigor. (Which protest to enter depends on whether one is addressing social scientists or ministers!)

Environment, like charity, covers a multitude of sins. I mean *sins* literally, for there is no possible means of drawing more than a theoretical line between the sins engendered by contact with an evil environment and those from an evil will. In broad outlines, one can say that a child reared in the slums is less responsible if he turns out a gangster than one reared in an educated, middle-class home; that one reared in domestic tension and exposed constantly to bickering is less to be blamed if he turns out badly than one whose environment is one of Christian culture. Such difference in responsibility it is necessary to recognize both for the sake of tolerance and of properly directed social change. Yet the fact remains that sin is sin—a stark reality and a humanly insurmountable barrier to the most effective living, however it gets engendered. The fact that so many people through their environment are predisposed not only to sin, but to lack the resources for spiritual mastery over sin, is one of the most baffling aspects of the entire metaphysical problem of evil.

Another obstacle both to the finding of salvation and to our power to live by it is our inescapable "groupism." The fact that we must live in groups is the mainspring of social security and social progress. Yet every blessing has its bane. Groupism, like the economic order, presents so many barriers to our spiritual freedom that I shall simply mention a few and pass on. Among the most important are: temptation of all sorts, rooting in the desire for the social approval; racialism and nationalism, increasingly recognized by ethically sensitive observers as Christianity's greatest rivals; class consciousness, which may be either a necessary step toward the securing of justice or in the form of class cleavages, one of the bitterest foes of love; traditionalism, which means essentially the hold of a linear, temporally-extended group upon the present; and finally the sheer complexity of group life. We are limited in our religious living by the mere fact (by no means "mere" in importance) that we live inevitably in so complicated, so unmanageable, so little understood, so unpredictable a society that even the best people are baffled either to know or do the will of God.

It is perniciously simple for those who have enough to eat and wear, a relatively secure position, a favorable heredity and cultural environment, and at least moderately good health to say that *anybody* ought to be able to rise above the limitations I have outlined. It is one of the most persistent fallacies of religious people to contend that if one has enough of the grace of God in his heart he can surmount any obstacle by spiritual transcendence of limitation. There is a great truth here which because of its greatness becomes the more dangerous when distorted. Through religious faith millions of people through the centuries have found spiritual victory over poverty, disease and the most untoward external circumstances. It is not good for anybody to get the idea that he cannot do so. But the fact remains that for great numbers of people such transcendence of physical and social limitation is impossible. It is impossible because this limitation has, from the start, so hampered their lives that they are unable either to see what God might do for them or make the spiritual self-surrender from which comes victory. "To him that hath shall be given" is both a divine promise and a haunting echo of demonic forces within the world.

3. OBSTACLES WITHIN

What of those forces within ourselves which thwart the possibility of our living on the level of triumphant religion? There is no clear dividing line here between inner and outer obstacles, for much that thwarts us from within can be traced to something from without. Some of these things we might have resisted had we tried; some we could not.

First, there is our inevitable provincialism. Of the selfish tendencies of human nature no more need be said except to call attention to the inescapable fact—inescapable in the best of us—that we are more interested in our own families, our own friends, our own professional associates, our own college, community or nation, than we can be in other persons outside of the circle of these interests. An American student could not possibly be as concerned about a war in Spain as about a war in which he might be called upon to enlist, or one in which his own brother or best friend might be killed.

The extent to which we can project ourselves outward to break over our provincialism is an important measure of the breadth and depth of Christian character. Even Jesus was tempted not to break over it but drawn irresistibly by human need he did so, as in his encounter with the Syro-Phœnician woman. The early church had to do this when the decision was made that Jews and Gentiles could have fellowship together. But it is needless to say how far we still are from escaping from narrow group loyalties. Since provincialism is an inverted form of the indispensable virtue of loyalty, we are not likely ever wholly to escape from it. Yet as long as we have it with us, it will block us from doing the will of God.

A second of these barriers is ignorance. Some of this

we could avoid by increased effort to be informed; some of it is our misfortune and not our fault. It is useless to expect that an uneducated middle-western farmer whose fields were being burned up with drought should understand very much or care very much about the political situation in Europe. He does not have to act in Europe, and he senses but dimly, or not at all, a connection between Europe and his affairs. Yet the same limitation of ignorance holds in regard to political affairs in his own country, where he has to act. It holds also in regard to such vital matters as the causes and cures of disease, unemployment and war. If a person knows the right thing to do he may not do it, but if he does not know it, the chances of his doing it are greatly diminished. It is these facts which nullify any argument which says that individual conversion is all that is needed for the remaking of society.

Perhaps an even more serious type of limitation through ignorance is in the field of religious knowledge. If a person has had a fundamentalist rearing and has worshiped always in a fundamentalist church under fundamentalist preaching, it is useless to expect him to have acquired any other framework of religious thought. That he cannot then readily unite his church religion and his school science is his misfortune but hardly his fault. Still more is this the case when he has grown up with no religious knowledge, and out of empty spaces tries suddenly to grasp some.

A third barrier is the binding power of habit. A genuine conversion with a consequent centering of life about a new focus is the most effective agent in breaking the hold of habit. But there are some habits so deeply imbedded in our neural patterns that neither human will nor divine grace can dislodge them. For example, drug addicts can sometimes be cured through religion when nothing else will work. But it would be sheer folly to believe that religion can give enough reinforcement of will to cure every drug addict. It is both a fairer judgment and a better strategy frankly to admit that some habits are too powerful to be broken, than to insinuate or suspect that a person who fails to live always on the upper levels of his aspirations was never converted. To make this charge without due knowledge is to "strike below the belt."

The conclusion to which we are led by this examination of barriers to triumphant religious living is one which was perhaps self-evident from the start—that to live the life of spiritual victory is no easy matter. There are signposts pointing toward knowledge of the will of God—yet places where for the most clear-seeing the signs become obscured by the pelting rains of existence. There are nourishing factors in the economic and social milieu which is the matrix of our being—yet for some, there is more of toxin than of nourishment. There are currents of life within us which keep us moving—yet everywhere are shallows which impede progress. Whether we look forward, around or within, we are forced to discover much which does not make for steady forward movement but for restless agitation.

Amid such confusion two things are to be done. One is

to look upward for such direction, such sustenance, such motive power as one does not find in the contemporary scene. The other is to clear away the impediments by as much of intelligently directed energy as can be mustered into action.

Chapter XVI

INVINCIBLE SURMISE

I. IN RETROSPECT

WE BEGAN this study by making some observations about the state of mind of youth who, deprived of their economic heritage, have become "the lost generation," and bereft of a religious heritage, are without inner stability or direction. We seem now to have come back to somewhere near our starting-point. But in the meantime we have swung around a rather large circle, and it may be well to pull together the main things which this book has tried to say.

The prevailing attitude of our present mores is a sense of the dissolution of life's meaning. This shows itself in a variety of ways—in a lack of response to the challenge of high enterprises, in a dulling of the sense of responsibility, in inner despair glossed over with a surface optimism, in all sorts of feverish activities by which to escape from looking at life's realities. The state of mind of this "lost" generation is traceable to many factors. Among them are the after-effects of four years of war and a decade of froth, irresponsibility bred through an educational system which both scatters energies and limits vision, failure to find connection between theoretical instruction and the demands of living, the seeping out of religious interest

as a backwash of philosophical and popular materialism, disintegration of the home both as a social institution and as a center of religious interest, failure of the
church to keep up with "the march of time."

Confronted with this situation, we must do something
about it—or let civilization go on the rocks through the
gradual dissolution of ideals in the lives of those who
make it up. Suggestions that we might trust nature and
wait, or change the environment, or supply inner supports through education, or evangelize people, all were
found to have in them valuable elements but to fall short
of offering much hope if any one of these ways were
trusted exclusively. This led to the suggestion of creative
idealism as a multiple approach. The remainder of the
book is an attempt to work out its implications.

With ideals thus placed in the foreground, it became
necessary to ask what there is in human nature which
justifies pinning hope upon their redemptive power. Man
is a creature of original sin and original goodness, of finitude and infinity. His most distinctive human trait—
and that which enables him to rise above besetting temptation and the turmoil of existence—is his capacity to
formulate ideals and live by them. This means the power
to regulate life by an inner non-coercive authority which
may, however, be used for high ends or low. It is within
man, yet acts with objective force.

This affirmation of the relevance of ideals to living
made it necessary to inquire further into their nature.
An ideal was defined as an idea made dynamic through
feeling, and therefore regulative upon action. Some are

and some are not attainable. All which determine conduct are psychologically real, though whether they are morally valid or cosmically grounded is another matter. All ideals have a moral foundation, and while moral ideals have a socio-biological origin it is necessary to guard against assuming that this explains them away—or says all there is to say about them.

By ideals man escapes from the acute unhappiness of a chaotic life, and in some measure from sin. Such escape may be on the level of prudential adjustment, or socially respected character, or triumphant religion. Religion may operate also within the second level, and it is there that the majority of religious people live. It is this fact that raises a question as to whether religion really makes a difference. On the third level no one need ask the question, for here religion visibly glorifies and transforms life.

If it is granted that to live on the level of triumphant religion, or active saintliness, is desirable, the next problem is how to achieve it. Here the question diverges into two channels, since both incarnation in life and the clarification of ideas are necessary. After a brief treatment of the former, the issues centering in the latter were discussed through several chapters.

The most important thing we have to do is to live greatly. But we are at once confronted by the problem of variability of judgment and lack of certainty in morals and religion. It is necessary, however, to distinguish between a practical certainty which is attainable in these fields by a sufficiently comprehensive view, and an absolute certainty which is neither attainable nor essential. An empirical approach, if our empiricism is radical enough, leads by the synoptic method to a supernaturalist conclusion. Truth and value are not to be confused, but neither is the road to truth through value to be spurned.

Confronted with the question of God's existence, we find evidences pointing in this direction. There is the authority of triumphant personal living, of history, of their meeting-point in Jesus Christ. The mystics' vision, whether in ecstasy or the milder and more dependable forms of communion, gives evidence not to be overlooked. So do the orderliness and progressive development of the world which science studies, although there are in it suggestions of limitation upon God's power. The moral imperative, heretofore affirmed more modestly, now is seen to converge with the argument from human personality to give evidence both of God's existence and of the cosmic reality of our higher ideals.

An inquiry into the nature of God led to denials that God is a man-like person, a force, an aspect of nature, or a process; it led to the affirmations that God is organizing mind, source and goal of ideals, cosmic companion, and poet of the universe. No study of the nature of God can be made apart from the problem of evil, and no examination of evil is dependable which fails to reckon with the problem of physical nature. These were examined with the conclusion that God is limited not only by human freedom and the orderly physical universe which he creates, but also by inertia in things and chance in events. Yet this does not prevent him from being able to "deliver us from evil" through spiritual triumph over tragedy.

Upon a human nature which cannot be viewed with any very optimistic outlook, God works to give redemption and power. To him who will look without self-deception at his sin and limitation, repent, and set his face forward and upward comes victory. By surrender of the freedom of self-will, a higher freedom is achieved. But this freedom is thwarted all along the way by difficulty of knowing the will of God, and by forces of colossal complexity and potency both around us and within. This calls for clear vision to judge action by the principle of the more inclusive good in the light of all the consequences; it calls for the most determined human effort to eliminate the barriers which hedge men in and lead to evil and frustrated living.

2. A CONTINUING CREED

What has been stated up to this point has made no claim to dispense with faith. Faith is indispensable to religious knowledge, as to every other form of knowledge by which we live. Yet thus far, I have tried to introduce nothing which could not rationally be justified on the grounds of a comprehensively empirical philosophy or theology.

In this concluding section, I shall suggest some things to which only the person predisposed to believe them through his Christian inheritance will be likely to assent. They are matters of great importance, but matters which lie in the realm of "the soul's invincible surmise."

I am constrained to say them, both because I believe them to be true, and because there is deep meaning for our day in these words of Goethe:

The deepest, nay, the unique theme of the history of the world, to which all other themes are subordinate, is the conflict of faith and unbelief. All epochs in which faith prevails—whatever its form may be—are noble, soul-elevating, and fruitful for the present and for after times. All epochs in which unbelief, be it under what form it may, wins an unhappy victory, even though for the moment they are invested with a deceptive halo of glory, vanish and are forgotten by posterity; because no one willingly wastes his pains on what is barren and unfruitful.[1]

I do not believe, and do not suppose the author of these words believed, that it makes no difference what kind of faith one has. It makes all the difference in the world. But that there should be some kind of faith to ennoble and make fruitful man's effort is the primary need for the present and the primary hope for the future.

This forward look will carry us into a backward look—into the great historic creeds of the Christian Church. The meaning of the incarnation, the cross, the resurrection and the ascension converge in the eternal fact of spiritual victory through the power of a God who manifests himself in human life, calls his followers to ways of suffering in devotion to ideals, triumphs over frustration and death, and lives in eternal glory. What this means for our day may be suggested in the form of a *credo*.

[1]"Noten zum Westöstlichen Divan" (1819) in *Goethes Werke*, ed. Heinemann, Vol. IV, p. 425.

I believe in a continuing incarnation—symbol of the eternal union of God with man. As God became flesh in Jesus of Nazareth and has manifested himself through the centuries to bring to man salvation through the Christ of faith, so must he be made manifest in us. The meaning of the greatest fact in history must ever be reenacted. The Word must again, and always, become flesh and dwell among us. Our light must shine among men to glorify the Father. Our darkness illumined by a living and eternal Christ, we ourselves in a true sense must become the light that lighteth every man that cometh into the world. If our light shine in darkness and the darkness comprehend it not, we must still bear witness.

I believe in a continuing cross—symbol of the eternal union of love with suffering. If we would be co-workers with God in the process of redemption, we must be prepared to meet obloquy and defeat, economic jeopardy, loneliness, perhaps even physical death. With a clear vision of the sin and weakness and also of the goodness and greatness of human nature, we must labor to remove those barriers which separate men from God and from their own best selves. Never doubting the power of God to redeem and heal, we must experience within ourselves that union of love with suffering which carried Jesus to Calvary.

I believe in a continuing resurrection—symbol of the eternal union of tragedy with triumph. In reliance upon the God whom Jesus worshiped and served we may share his confidence in the deathlessness of our enterprise, knowing that "what is excellent, as God lives, is permanent." We may rest also in the assurance that man's spirit, the candle of the Lord, will not be snuffed out in stench and its clear light brought to nothing when the body is no longer seen.

I believe in a continuing ascension—symbol of the union of temporal with eternal values. The resurrection upon this planet points to something which lies beyond, not deathless only, but timeless. Ascension through sacrifice to glory—not the self-glorification which is sin but the divine glory—is the way of the cross and the way of conquest. We express this deep-lying truth when we sing:

> In the cross of Christ I glory,
> Towering o'er the wrecks of time.

All that matters upon earth may go to defeat, and the battle still be won in the glory which is life eternal.

Such victory, whether temporal or eternal, may be won in a day when ideals are shattered and men, lost and bewildered, are ready to surrender. Those who labor for the ideals which make for triumphant living have the resources of God upon their side, and in this confidence it is possible "to build above the deep intent the deed."

APPENDIX

READERS interested in pursuing further the implications of the theory of creation outlined in Chapter XIII may wish to have a more extended statement of God's relation to each element in it.

Human persons and physical things are created by God and depend for their existence upon him. In this I assent to the usual Christian concept of creation except in two respects: (1) that I believe creation to be an eternal process, (2) that I regard things as having a measure of independence of action (not panpsychistic or consciously chosen freedom) by virtue of the fact that they are not merely things, but also events in a system of events some of which are fortuitous.

Such unwilled events are not to be thought of as something uncaused or self-caused. Every event happens because a person, a thing, or a combination of personal and physical agency causes it to happen. But to say that an event is *caused* is not the equivalent of saying that it is *willed*. In the total nexus of events, circumstances emerge which bring about events willed by neither God nor man.

Events are in part but not wholly dependent on God's will. Events exist in an orderly system, the order of which is to be ascribed to God's creating in conformity to eternal principles of rationality. *But it is not a closed system.* Within the system is spontaneity which may take the form of (1) the purposeful activity of God in the direction of higher values, (2) the free activity of man, directed toward good or evil ends, (3) the morally neutral, unwilled juxtaposition of circumstances which I have called inertia in things and chance in events. The last type, the crux of my theory of evil in so far as it differs from that of liberal theism, gives rise to events which *as events* are outside of God's control, yet God has unlimited resources to impart to men for bringing spiritual victory out of any situation arising from them.

The forms also are in part but not wholly dependent on God's will, though in a quite different sense from the events. God does not create his own attributes; to be rational and good he conforms to eternally given structures of rationality and goodness which are an integral element of his nature but not made by him. He is thus limited by *form* and without form "was not anything made that hath been made." The specific *forms* which characterize the created universe in its manifold aspects, though eternal possibilities, become actual only as creativity takes place and they depend upon God, the "maker of heaven and earth," for their existence.

The view which I have outlined is in one sense pluralistic and in another monistic. God and human persons are quantitatively separate centers of conscious activity. Minds, things, events, and forms are *qualitatively different,* yet *organically interrelated,* aspects of reality. My position is dualistic only in the sense that I regard the value-thwarting processes of the universe to be, as historical events, partially independent of God's control. Yet monism in the most important sense is saved if God has unlimited power to aid men in spiritual transcendence over evil.

The question as to whether God's purposes in the created order may not ultimately be thwarted depends on whether "ultimately" is conceived temporally or in terms of spiritual meaning. I see no reason to suppose that a condition of static perfection will ever be achieved upon earth and within the field of history. History gives evidence that a progressive achievement of good has actually taken place; the Christian Gospel presents an obligation to work for the coming of the Kingdom of God upon earth, and a hope that this will increasingly come to pass. But the Christian life, whether in the individual or society, is always a quest with more beyond. In this sense there is no ultimate (*i.e.,* completed) victory. Yet at every moment spiritual victory is possible. Religion is "anticipated attainment"—an apprehension of divine, eternal, limitless, personal power in the midst of human weakness and sin. In the latter sense there need be no fear that God will not ultimately triumph; for he triumphs already—and always —in the fullest sense, and thereby enables men to bring meaning and value out of chaos. Should everything upon earth and the earth itself be extinguished in chaos, there would still be immortality—and a God whose being and power do not depend upon men's strivings.

BOOKS SUGGESTED FOR FURTHER READING

The following list is in no sense a complete bibliography. It is intended as a suggestion of some of the most valuable books to be read by those who are interested in pursuing further the major themes discussed in this volume:

Bennett, John C., *Social Salvation*.
——, *Christianity—and Our World*.
Unusually clear and well-balanced statements of a Christian social philosophy.

Brightman, Edgar S., *Is God a Person?*
——, *Personality and Religion*.
Compact and interesting expositions of the author's personalistic philosophy, with valuable discussions of the nature of God and his relations to the world.

Brown, William Adams, *Pathways to Certainty*.
Appropriately named.

Calhoun, Robert L., *God and the Common Life*.
Difficult but rewarding, especially the chapter on the nature of God.

Fosdick, Harry Emerson, *Adventurous Religion*.
Easily read. One of the best popular statements of liberal theology.

Hocking, William Ernest, *The Meaning of God in Human Experience*.
——, *Human Nature and Its Remaking*.
Outstanding classics. To be read slowly and pondered.

Horton, Walter M., *Theism and the Modern Mood.*
——, *A Psychological Approach to Theology.*
——, *Realistic Theology.*
    Writtten with clarity and insight.

Jones, Rufus M., *Pathways to the Reality of God.*
——, *The Testimony of the Soul.*
    The first discusses various approaches, the second mainly that through ethical and spiritual intuition.

Jung, Carl G., *Modern Man in Search of a Soul.*
    A vigorous portrayal of the importance of religion by one of the world's greatest psychologists.

Lewis, Edwin G., *God and Ourselves.*
    A scholarly and religiously vital treatment of important problems in the philosophy of religion.

Luccock, Halford E., *Christian Faith and Economic Change.*
——, *Christianity and the Individual.*
    Anything by this author has both literary charm and religious insight.

Lyman, Eugene W., *The Meaning and Truth of Religion.*
    Comprehensive. Of lasting value.

Macmurray, John, *The Structure of Religious Experience.*
    An important humanistic interpretation of religion in terms of community.

Montague, William P., *Belief Unbound.*
    A challenging defense of a limited God by a philosopher who, unlike most of those mentioned in this list, is not a theologian.

Niebuhr, Reinhold, *Moral Man and Immoral Society.*
——, *An Interpretation of Christian Ethics.*
    Not easily understood, but worth making an effort to grasp.

Tillich, Paul, *The Religious Situation.*
    A penetrating analysis by a great German scholar, now in exile in America.

Van Dusen, Henry P., *The Plain Man Seeks for God.*
——, *God in These Times.*
  The first, less simple than it sounds, is an excellent treatment
    of the philosophy of religion; the second is among the best
    of many discussions of the present religious outlook.

Whitehead, Alfred N., *Religion in the Making.*
——, *Adventures of Ideas.*
  Relatively understandable, charmingly written presentations
    of a profound philosophy which has great religious sig-
    nificance.

Wieman, Henry N., and Regina Westcott-Wieman, *A Nor-
    mative Psychology of Religion.*
  Well worth reading for its psychology even if its philosophy
    is not accepted.

Wright, William K., *A Students' Philosophy of Religion.*
  A standard text which includes the history and psychology
    as well as the philosophy of religion.

INDEX

INDEX

Abrams, R., 200
Acquisitiveness, 23, 41, 133, 139
Adjustment, prudential, 58–60, 102, 217
Alternation, principle of, 117
American Youth Commission, 4
Anaxagoras, 95
Animal pain, 175
Anthropomorphism, 135 f., 142, 183
Art, 52, 80 f., 158 f., 170
Ascension, the, 220, 222
Atonement, the, 111
Augustine, St., 33, 38, 114
Authority, as approach to knowledge, 84, 92 ff., 95, 103, 121; as evidence of God, 105–113, 133, 218; of history, 109–111, 121, 133, 218; of Jesus, 111–113, 121, 133, 218; of personality, 107–109, 121, 133, 218; inner non-coercive, 39, 57, 186, 191, 216

Barthian theology, 189, 192
Behaviorism, 18
Berkeley, G., 144 n., 173 n.
Bible, 76, 84, 95, 107 ff., 125, 149, 193, 200
Biological evolution, 94–96, 125–127
Brightman, E. S., 162 f.
Bryan, W. J., 96, 98, 124

Cadman, S. P., 108
Calvin, J., 199
Capitalism, 71, 207
Carneades, 86
Causality, 125, 160, 177
Certainty, degrees of, 87, 90; practical and absolute, 84–90, 97, 103, 217; subjective, 116, 122
Chance, 130, 163, 171, 176, 179 f., 185, 218

Character, socially respected, 60–62, 68, 102, 217
Church, and college, 8, 20–22; defects of, 21; loyalty to, 7, 61
Circumstance, juxtapositions of, 124, 166, 171, 179, 223
Clinchy, E., 200
Coherence, 82, 93, 96 f., 118
Communism, 6
Conditioning, 53, 55, 138, 186
Conscience, 39 f., 53 ff., 132
Conversion, 192–197, 212
Creation, 139, 145, 152, Ch. XIII, 223–225
Creeds, 107 ff., 157
Cross, the, 68 n., 181, 220 ff.

Damien, Father, 62
Darrow, C., 124
Darwin, C., 94
Davis, M., 2, 3, 8
Death, 24, 40, 43, 176 ff.
Deism, 140 f.
Depression, effects of, 2–12; in morale, 3
Descartes, R., 84 f.
Determinism, 18 f., 208
Devil, 159, 184
Dissolution of ideals, Ch. I, 215; causes of, 13–22, 215; remedies for, 22–29
Divine grace, 26, 36, 145, 194, 198, 213
Dualism, 180, 224

Economic barriers to religious living, 207; exploitation, 200; insecurity, 2 ff.
Ecstasy, mystical, 114–116, 121, 133, 218
Education, effects on ideals, 14–17, 25–27, 215 f.
Egocentricity, 33 f., 37 f., 68 n., 101

233

INDEX

Paul, St., 38, 131, 187–190
Personalism, 163 f.
Personality, as ethical norm, 83, 155, 201–203; as evidence of God, 107–109, 130 f., 141, 218; Christian, 62–77; nature of, Ch. III, 141
Plato, 33, 36 n., 69, 152, 201
Plotinus, 114
Pluralism, 224
Poet, God as, 156–158
Pragmatic test, 79, 93 f., 103, 105, 117 f.
Prayer, 27, 73 f., 102, 116, 124, 148, 200
Predestination, 192
Prevailing states of mind, 4–12
Pride, spiritual, 27, 154, 222
Profit motive, 23
Progressive education, 14
Prophets, 67, 129, 149
Pseudo-Dionysius, 114
Psychiatry, 12, 18
Psychological basis of ideals, Ch. III, 53 ff.
Psychology of religion, 18; physiological, 54

Racialism, 200, 209
Radicalism in colleges, 7
Realism, theistic, 165
Reality, types of, 164 ff., 184
Redemption, 72, 134, 185, 191, 219
Religion, and science, 16, 81; excluded from homes, 20; excluded from schools, 15; meaning of, 30, 225; triumphant, 29, 62–65, Ch. VI, 102 f., 108, 117, 185, 191, 210, 217
Religious education, 76, 137, 192; experience, 27, 113–120, 185; knowledge, Chs. VII, VIII, 219; living, barriers to, 46, 131, Ch. XIV, 219, 221
Repentance, 194, 219
Resurrection, 220 f.

Revelation, 32 n., 84, 98 f., 103, 149, 193, 198, 203
Rousseau, J. J., 36
Russell, B., 19, 124

Saintliness, 64 ff., 205, 217
Salvation, 46 f., 57, 58, 102, Ch. XIV, 198; barriers to, Ch. XV; meaning of, 191 f.; method of, 192–197
Santayana, G., 85
Schweitzer, A., 62
Science, 52, 80 f., 83 f., 93, 95, 103, 105; and religion, 16, 81, 119; as evidence of God, 122–129, 134, 141, 218
Secularism, Chs. I, II, 72
Security, 2 ff., 59
Self-realization, 201 ff.
Servetus, M., 199
Shakespeare, W., 26, 54
Sin, 23, 26, 29, 101, 128 f., 221; and the problem of evil, 158 ff., 175, 184; and salvation, Ch. XIV, 217, 219; as maladjustment, 18; conviction of, 193; forgiveness of, 194 f.; loss of sense of, 68, 72; nature of, 35, 38; original, 32–36, 110, 186; social, 207 f.
Skepticism, 82, 86
Smith, Joseph, 199
Social sciences, 1, 17–19, 110, 127 ff., 208
Society of Friends, 27
Socrates, 26, 36, 69, 201
Sorley, W. R., 27 n.
Spinoza, B., 144
Spontaneity in nature, 123, 171, 173, 175–180, 223
Stoicism, 64, 202
Student Volunteer Movement, 9
Suffering, problem of, 124, 126, 158–163, 174–182; redemptive power of, 74 f., 102

236